Society American Anti-Slavery

Annual report of the American Anti-Slavery Society

By the executive committee, for the year ending May 1, 1859.

Society American Anti-Slavery

Annual report of the American Anti-Slavery Society
By the executive committee, for the year ending May 1, 1859.

ISBN/EAN: 9783744738675

Printed in Europe, USA, Canada, Australia, Japan

Cover: Foto ©Suzi / pixelio.de

More available books at **www.hansebooks.com**

ANNUAL REPORT

OF THE

American Anti-Slavery Society,

BY THE EXECUTIVE COMMITTEE,

FOR THE

YEAR ENDING MAY 1, 1859.

NEW YORK:

AMERICAN ANTI-SLAVERY SOCIETY,

No. 5 Beekman Street.

1860.

OFFICERS

OF THE

AMERICAN ANTI-SLAVERY SOCIETY,

ELECTED MAY, 1859.

PRESIDENT.

WILLIAM LLOYD GARRISON, MASSACHUSETTS.

VICE PRESIDENTS.

PETER LIBBEY, Maine.	THOMAS WHITSON, Pennsylvania.
LUTHER MELENDY, New Hampshire.	JOSEPH MOORE, "
JOHN M. HAWKS, " "	ROWLAND JOHNSON, New Jersey.
JEHIEL C. CLAFLIN, Vermont.	ALFRED GIBBS CAMPBELL, "
FRANCIS JACKSON, Massachusetts.	THOMAS GARRETT, Delaware.
EDMUND QUINCY, "	THOMAS DONALDSON, Ohio.
ASA FAIRBANKS, Rhode Island.	SARAH OTIS ERNST, "
JAMES B. WHITCOMB, Connecticut.	BENJAMIN BOWN, "
SAMUEL J. MAY, New York.	WILLIAM HEARN, Indiana.
CORNELIUS BRAMHALL, " "	WILLIAM HOPKINS, "
AMY POST, " "	JOSEPH MERRITT, Michigan.
PLINY SEXTON, " "	THOMAS CHANDLER, "
LYDIA MOTT, " "	CYRUS FULLER, "
LUCRETIA MOTT, Pennsylvania.	CARVER TOMLINSON, Illinois.
ROBERT PURVIS, "	CALEB GREEN, Minnesota.
EDWARD M. DAVIS, "	GEORGIANA B. KIRBY, California.

CORRESPONDING SECRETARY.

CHARLES C. BURLEIGH, PLAINFIELD, CT.

RECORDING SECRETARY.

WENDELL PHILLIPS, BOSTON.

TREASURER.

FRANCIS JACKSON, BOSTON.

EXECUTIVE COMMITTEE.

WILLIAM LLOYD GARRISON.	ANNE WARREN WESTON.
FRANCIS JACKSON.	SYDNEY HOWARD GAY.
EDMUND QUINCY.	SAMUEL MAY, JR.
MARIA WESTON CHAPMAN.	WILLIAM I. BOWDITCH.
WENDELL PHILLIPS.	CHARLES K. WHIPPLE.
ELIZA LEE FOLLEN.	HENRY C. WRIGHT.

REPORT FOR 1858-9.

THE Executive Committee of the American Anti-Slavery Society have now to add the history of another year to the annals of the Anti-Slavery enterprise.

KANSAS.

During this year the Kansas question seems to have reached its solution; so far, at least, as to put beyond a reasonable doubt the defeat of the attempt to make a Slave State of the Territory. At the date of our last Report, the issue immediately pending was, whether Kansas would accept the "Ordinance" proposed by the traitor, ENGLISH, and be thereupon at once admitted to the Union as a Slaveholding State, under the Lecompton Constitution; or would reject it, and take such chance as might remain of coming in as a Free State. The second day of last August, (being that of the Missouri State election, and therefore one on which the Border Ruffians would be busy at home,) was wisely chosen by the Free State officials of Kansas for the taking of the vote on that issue. The result was a most emphatic rejection of the Ordinance, and, consequently of the Lecompton abomination. For accepting, there were hardly two thousand votes; and nearly twelve thousand for rejecting. The meaning of such a response, given in spite of the strenuous efforts of the General Government and its partisans to secure a different result, could not easily be honestly mistaken; and though some unscrupulous politicians pretended to see in it only a proof of the unwillingness of Kansas to become a State at present, yet it was doubtless in reality everywhere well understood as expressing her abhorrence of the Lecompton Constitution, and her fixed determination to keep the curse of chattel Slavery from her soil. So when the President's organ, the Washington *Union*, says, "the vexed question of Slavery had little or nothing to do with the decision," all we understand by the assertion is, that the Washington *Union* has little or nothing to do with truth and honesty, where the interests of its party and its liege lord, the Slave Power, are concerned.

In the greater part of the Territory the Free State men have become so decidedly the stronger party that open violence is no longer attempted against them; but in the southern counties, where they are less numerous, the old methods are still, at times employed, with intent to drive them out. At intervals, throughout the year, that part of the Territory has been the theatre of civil war, or something very like it; and of atrocities hardly surpassed by those of any former period in the history of Kansas. Gangs of marauders, composed in part of the more violent Pro-Slavery men of the Territory, and in part of their Missourian allies, have ranged the country, robbing, burning, and murdering; and the Free State men, finding themselves unprotected by the Government, armed and organized in self-defence, and at times made reprisals upon their adversaries, with such energy and effect, that the names of their principal leaders, MONTGOMERY, and JOHN BROWN of Ossawattomie, became a terror in all the haunts of Border Ruffianism. The most signal achievement of the Ruffians, during the year, was the massacre, in cold blood, of a number of peaceable Free State men, who had taken no part in any of the conflicts of physical force, but had moderately opposed the establishment of Slavery in Kansas, and had voted against the Lecompton Constitution. The murderers, twenty-five or thirty in number, mounted and armed, (and most of them from Missouri,) came, on the 19th of May, to the "Trading Post," in Linn county, seized eleven men unarmed and unsuspicious of danger, some of them at work in their fields, some travelling with their teams on the highway, and others in their stores or houses, — took them into a secluded ravine, drew them up in a line, and deliberately shot them down. Five were killed,

and five severely wounded; one escaped unhurt by falling with
the rest and feigning death. After plundering their victims. the
murderers fled in haste to Missouri, and were over the line before
the people of the region — intensely excited by news of the
massacre, and promptly gathering for pursuit — could overtake
them. Nothing has been done, either by the General Government or by that of Missouri, toward having them arrested and
brought to justice, although the names of nearly all of them
were known; and their leaders, in particular, had already become notorious by former bloody deeds in the service of Slavery.
How much, indeed, can be expected from the General Government, in the way of aiding to vindicate law or justice against
those who outrage both by the methods they employ to subju-
gate free territory to Slavery, we may infer from the President's
appointment, about that time, of the notorious murderer, CLARK
— well known as one of the bloodiest agents of the Slave
Power in its war against Kansas — to the office of purser in the
navy. The massacre did, however, arouse Governor DENVER;
so that, it is said, in the first heat of excitement, he talked
strongly of what should be done about it, and spoke of a requisition upon the Governor of Missouri for its perpetrators; but
we do not learn that he ever sent one, or if he did, that any
notice was taken of it.

DENVER, like his predecessors, seems to have begun his administration with a strong leaning to the Pro-Slavery party; but in
its progress, to have undergone, like them, a change of feeling,
as he became better acquainted with the real state of affairs;
till at length, having found, probably, as they had done, that the
task set at Washington for a Governor of Kansas was too hard
for a man with a conscience or a decent self-respect, or a regard for the esteem of honest men, he resigned in about nine
months after his appointment. A little while before his resig-
nation he visited the seat of war in the southern counties, and
by his mediation a compromise was effected between the contending parties; both agreeing to refrain from all attempts to
avenge or punish alleged offences past, of either against the
other; and to await the action of the regular authorities touching all matters of complaint. But the Pro-Slavery party soon
broke the agreement, by treacherously seizing a Free State man
and confining him in Fort Scott, the Border Ruffian strong-

hold; to be tried on an indictment previously found against him by a packed Grand Jury, for some act done before the compromise. They induced him to yield quietly to the arrest by pretending it was on a charge of some slight offence against the law, of which, as he was known to be innocent, he expected a speedy acquittal; and by solemnly assuring him that he should be held and tried on no other charge. When he was fully in their power, they told him their real design, menacing him with death, as the penalty of the offence alleged against him. Hearing of this breach of faith, the Free State people first tried peaceful negotiation for the prisoner's release; and that failing, MONTGOMERY, with seventy resolute men, came upon Fort Scott by surprise early in the morning of December 16th, and after a brief struggle, rescued him by force, killing one of the Pro-Slavery men in the fight. Immediately thereafter, messengers were sent to Lecompton to procure the aid of the Federal troops against MONTGOMERY and his associates; and meetings were held in Missouri, all along the border, to concert measures and enlist men for an invasion of Southern Kansas. The more timid of the Free State men, alarmed by the threats of the Missourians, began to leave the Territory, or to remove to the northern part of it, beyond the reach of the apprehended danger. But the bolder spirits met the menace in another way — by an inroad into Missouri; showing the threateners that if they *would* have war, they could have it at home, and need not seek it elsewhere. Having learned that a family of Slaves near the line were soon to be sold, and wished for help to escape, two small companies, one of them led by "OLD BROWN," went over on the night of December 20th, liberated those Slaves and several others, and took two prisoners, whom, however, they released and sent back after bringing them some distance into the Territory. BROWN's party achieved their purpose without bloodshed; but a Slaveholder was killed by the other party, while fighting against the liberation of his Slave. The liberated Slaves accompanied their deliverers to the Territory, and thence made their way safely to Canada, in spite of an attempt by the Missourians to intercept their flight.

After this fresh taste of the quality of their antagonists, the Missourians abandoned the contemplated invasion, thinking, no doubt, that it would be wiser to employ less perilous methods of annoyance and revenge. A committee was sent to the Governor of the State to try to get from him a requisition upon the Governor of Kansas for Brown and his associates. Rewards for the arrest of Montgomery and Brown were offered by the Governor of Missouri and President Buchanan. Medary, the new Governor of Kansas, sent officers into the disturbed region, to try the efficacy of legal authority in composing the troubles. But indifferent success attended these measures. It was found impracticable, or imprudent at least, to arrest the dreaded Free State leaders; so nobody ventured to earn the promised rewards; and as no attempt was made to execute the law upon the Ruffians, whose aggressions had provoked resistance and reprisal, and no rewards were offered for their arrest, the Free State people naturally enough insisted on their own right of self-protection, till the Government should show itself both able and willing to guarantee them safety for the future, if not satisfaction for the past.

In February, the Territorial Legislature passed, and the Governor approved, a general amnesty for all past offences growing out of the partisan strife in the southern counties. But hardly yet is the condition of those counties one of assured tranquillity.

The Legislature also passed an Act requiring the people to vote, on the last Monday in March, upon the question of calling a Convention to frame a new Constitution for a State Government. In case of an affirmative vote, delegates to the Convention are to be chosen on the 7th of June, and are to meet for their work on the 7th of July; the Constitution is to be submitted to the people on the 4th of October; and, if it is ratified, the election for State officers under it is to be held on the 6th of December. The vote in March having been, by nearly six to one in favor of calling the Convention, it is probable that the other steps will be taken in due succession, and that Kansas will present herself, at the next session of Congress, for admission into the Union, with a Constitution framed and adopted with unimpeachable regularity, and acknowledged on all hands to embody the will of a majority of her people.

Near the close of its session, the Legislature passed an Act abolishing Slavery in the Territory, but by some trickery, in which the Governor was suspected of having a part, it was kept from reaching him till so late an hour that simply by his not returning it, with either approval or veto, it failed to become a law. It was believed that he purposely shunned the responsibility of a distinct expression either way, from a fear that approval of the bill would offend his masters at Washington, and that an express veto would lessen his chances of preferment by the people of Kansas when in the Union. That the bill was no piece of superfluous legislation is evident, not only from Judicial and Presidential assertions of the legal existence of Slavery in the Territory, but also from the actual advertising of Slave property for sale by a Territorial officer. Such a disgraceful fact as this last mentioned was hardly needed, it is true, to prove that the Slave Power is always thoroughly in earnest in its theoretical assumptions, and means to put them into practice to the full reach of its ability. But it may help to keep this already well-established truth fresh in the memory of those —and they are quite too many—who are wont to forget it just when it ought especially to be remembered, and so are ever ready to be deceived by some new pretence of compromise between the rights of Freedom and the demands of Slavery.

At intervals, during the last few months, the Missourians and their allies in the Territory have diversified their operations with attempts at kidnapping; sometimes with but too much success. In the latter part of August, a Creek Indian, living at Quindaro, was seized a few miles from that place, by an armed band from Missouri, hurried across the border, and lodged in the jail at Independence, on the charge that he had been running at large in Missouri without an owner, though he had free papers from the Indian agent in Kansas, and had not been within ten miles of the Missouri line. When the outrage was known, the people were much excited, and a lawyer promptly went down to Independence, to take legal measures for the man's release, but we have not been able to learn with what result. A correspondent of the Albany *Journal*, writing in the early part of November, says that "a number of Missourians and others have been combining to kidnap free colored persons doing business in Lawrence, some as barbers and others as wood-cutters; also three women. But after the escape of one of the men from his bonds with which they had bound him, also another jumping out of a hack at night, and being shot at on making his escape, the parties have been arrested. Some of them *belong to the post-office.* They will most likely be bound over for trial before Judge ELMORE, an appointee of President BUCHANAN," and — another proof that Slavery needs abolishing there — " the largest Slaveowner in Kansas."

The Lawrence *Republican* gives particulars of two cases, (probably among those mentioned by the writer just quoted,) which occurred on two successive evenings near the beginning of November. In one, a laborer returning from his day's work in the city to his home near it, was stopped by three men, threatened with death if he cried out, bound and conveyed in a wagon to a house near Franklin, and confined there that night and the next day. The next night he contrived to loosen his bonds, jumped from a second story window, and escaped. In the other, CHARLES FISHER — a barber, living a little way out of the city, while walking home early in the evening — was overtaken by three or four men in a hack. Just after passing him, one of them got out, drew a pistol, and told him to stop or he would kill him. FISHER ran back toward a house near by; the kidnappers followed and shot at him, but seeing that the owner of the house had come out and was running to meet them, they turned and drove furiously toward Franklin. Next morning the driver of the hack was arrested and bound over for trial; but, when the case came on, Judge ELMORE, true to a Slaveholder's instincts, and as became an officer appointed by President BUCHANAN, released him on the ground that persons of African descent cannot be admitted to testify against a white man. " The decision," as the *Republican* justly adds, " is equivalent to declaring that there is no law in the Territory against the kidnapping of colored persons; for, in the very nature of the case, the witnesses must, in almost every such case, be the injured parties themselves."

About two months later FISHER was seized again, — this time at Leavenworth, two police men of that city aiding in the crime. They came upon him while asleep in his shop, at night, and by threatening to shoot him through the window, compelled him to rise and let them in; then pretending a charge of theft against him, handcuffed him, took him to the river — telling those whom his cries brought out to see what was the matter, that it was only an Irishman arrested for fighting — put him into a boat, and rowed across to Missouri. But the next

2

night he escaped, with handcuffs on, found a skiff, crossed the river, and not without peril of drowning, reached the Kansas shore. "A large meeting was held to welcome him back, and it was agreed on all hands that he was worthy of freedom." The Missourians, however, were bent on having him, and he was soon after taken again, on a regular warrant, as a fugitive from service, and committed to prison to await examination; whereupon a writ of habeas corpus was procured by his friends, and, resistance being offered to its service, the sheriff broke down the door of the room in which he was confined, and he was released and carried off in triumph.

On the very day, January 25th, on which this rescue was effected, an outrage was perpetrated exceeding all of a like kind which had preceded it. It was the kidnapping of Dr. Doy and his son, with another white man, named CLOUGH, and thirteen colored men and women, whom they were conducting across the country from a too perilous nearness to the Missouri border. The people of Lawrence, at a meeting held doubtless in consequence of the repeated attempts to kidnap their colored fellow-citizens, had decided to assist them in removing to a safer distance from the haunts of the man-stealers; and had prevailed upon Dr. Doy to take charge of their removal. Of those who composed his company, all had free papers except two, and these were free born — one a native of Ohio, the other of Pennsylvania. Of those who had been Slaves, the Lawrence *Republican* states that one woman had been sent to Kansas by her own mistress, to put her beyond the reach of her master and his two sons, for reasons which we need not name.

The company, in two large wagons, had gone about ten or twelve miles, when they were suddenly surprised and surrounded by a band of armed and mounted men, mostly Missourians, but some of them citizens of Kansas. Foremost among them were the Mayor and the Marshal of Weston, Mo., and the Postmaster of Lawrence. Stopping the wagons, they offered to pay Dr. Doy well if he would drive to Leavenworth; but, upon his replying that his team should never take a man into Slavery, several of them dismounted, put their pistols to his head, bound him and all his companions, took the horses, wagons, money and other property, (he protesting against their acts as kidnapping and highway robbery,) put on drivers, and keeping scouts in front and rear, drove with headlong speed toward Missouri, till one wagon broke down; then threw out the baggage, packed all their prisoners into the other wagon, and again hurried on. Reaching Leavenworth at night, they passed through the town stealthily, and rode to the ferry, where the boat was waiting with steam up, ready to take them across. The prisoners were ordered aboard on pain of being shot. Dr. Doy refused to go till guns were pointed at him, and he was told his life and property would both be lost unless he went; while Wood, the Mayor of Weston, and many others, promised upon their honor, that if he would go he should return all safe and sound in the morning. He then went with the rest, and their landing in Weston was greeted with the firing of salutes and other tokens of rejoicing, and all possible insults were offered to the captives. They were thrown upon the floor of the police office, and lay there the remainder of the night. In the morning, the Weston *Argus* issued a jubilant Extra, duly garnished with falsehood, "that the country might have all the facts just as they were, before the howling misrepresentations of the Abolitionists should poison the Northern atmosphere." The Doctor and his white companions were taken to the court house for examination, amid insulting shouts of the people; their request for delay of a day or two to procure counsel was denied; and they were committed for trial, bail being fixed at $5000; in default of which the Doctor and his son were sent to Platte city jail, but CLOUGH was released, probably with the hope of buying him up as a witness against the other two. While the case was before the examining court, Dr. DOY wrote a protest, as a citizen of Kansas, against the whole proceeding, but it was of course disregarded by the judicial tools of the kidnappers.

Some of the colored prisoners were given up to persons claiming to be their masters; others, who were free born, even according to the Slave code, and would not admit that they were Slaves, were thrust into prison, doubtless to await sufficiently unscrupulous claimants, or, in due time, to be sold for their jail fees. Two of these, the men above-mentioned, as natives of Ohio and Pennsylvania, after being about a week in jail, were taken out by one of the kidnappers, "the notorious fiend, JAKE HURD, of Lecompton," so called in Dr. Doy's letter, from which most of these particulars are drawn. When told to go with him, they said they would wait in prison till their free papers came. He replied, with an oath, that he was their master now, and would make them obey him, then whipped them till they consented to go.

The treatment of Dr. Doy and his son was in keeping with all the rest of the proceedings. They were — to use his own words — confined in an eight feet square iron box, having to burn fat meat to make light by night or day;" had "no water to wash with," and, when his letter was writte.., had seen no one whom they knew since the day of their imprisonment. Men from Kansas had gone over to learn their condition and to demand their release, but were not permitted to see them.

As will be readily supposed, the news of this outrage caused a strong excitement in the Territory. It was vehemently denounced, not without menaces of unpleasant consequences to the Missouri border, if the prisoners should not be released unharmed.

At the meeting of Congress, in December last, the President devoted a large space in his Annual Message to the affairs of Kansas; persisting with the cool assurance of a practiced falsifier, in misrepresenting the well known facts of its history, and slandering that great majority of its people who have given him and his master, the Slave Power, such grave offence, by refusing to submit to lawless usurpation, thinly disguised under the stolen *forms* of law. With mingled cant of piety and of patriotism — for what but cant is pious and patriotic talk prefacing sophistry and falsehood, uttered in the interest of oppression, violence, and fraud? — he began by comparing the condition of the country at that time with what it was one year before, and affected to see "much reason for gratitude to that Almighty Providence which has never failed to interpose for our relief at the most critical period of our history." Just precisely for what he was moved to give thanks; whether that the Lecompton villany had not achieved the full success which at the previous session he strained every nerve to win; or that it was saved by the basest treachery from the prompt and crushing defeat it merited; as he did not specify, so there was no need that he should. How acceptable to the "Almighty Providence" is gratitude called forth by the partial success or seeming impunity of wickedness; or with what measure of complacency He hears himself accused, (under the guise of thankful acknowledgment,) of having interposed to relieve a nation of oppressors, and a corrupt and iniquitous government from the dangers and disasters consequent upon their sins, which they refuse either to repent of or forsake, we trust that we as little need to be informed.

The President was "happy to say" that "much has been done, during the last session of Congress, toward " accomplishing the object of "every patriot's desire," to "remove the excitement" about Kansas "from the States, and confine it to the Territory." But he did not say — probably because it is a truth he would not have been "happy" to tell — that, so far as this end was approached, it was through the partial defeat of his cherished scheme, and the confidence thus, and by other means, inspired among the friends of Freedom, that the final victory of their cause was sure; whereas, if he had been able as he was desirous to press through Congress his pet measure for forcing upon Kansas a Constitution justly abhorred by five-sixths of her people, "the excitement" in "the States," and the Territory too, would have been more intense than ever. By omitting this truth, even the truth which he did tell, was made to convey, as he evidently meant it should, the falsehood by implication, that whatever tranquillizing effect had followed the action of Congress, was due to measures which he had proposed or approved.

Nor was he content with falsehood by implication. He affirmed that "the principle has been recognized in some form or other by an almost unanimous vote of both Houses of Congress, that a Territory has a right to come into the Union either as a Free or a Slave State, according to the will of a majority of its people." That principle has *not* been so recognized. No doubt the "Lecompton Democrats" meant all that in voting for the Ruffian Constitution; and possibly, the "Anti-Lecompton Democrats" would allow their vote for the CRITTENDEN or MONTGOMERY substitute to be so interpreted, though we doubt if they all would. But both these made up only a small majority of the House, and by no means enough to give "an almost unanimous vote" in the Senate. The Republican members, therefore, must be counted in to make the vote "almost unanimous in both Houses;" and the President unquestionably meant

to claim them as recognizing "the principle" he stated. If he
did not, he spoke untruly as to the strength of the vote. If
he did, he charged the Republicans falsely. It was well known
from the tenor of their speeches, from the tone of the press
of their party, and from their course in the whole controversy —
that they never meant to admit "that a Territory has *a right*
to come into the Union as a Free or a Slave State." The President could hardly have been so ignorant of their position and
views as honestly to misapprehend the meaning of their votes.
He must have known — as we presume every body else did —
that they voted to let Kansas into the Union with a Constitution of her own choice, because they *knew* her choice would be
to come in as a Free State; and that such a vote does not imply a willingness to admit a Slave State or one likely to be such;
nor does it recognize a *right* in such a State, or indeed in any
State, even Kansas itself, to come in.   If a mercantile firm takes
in a new partner of approved integrity and capacity, the act will
hardly be construed, even by JAMES BUCHANAN, to imply that
any one who may wish it, rogue or honest man, capable or incapable, has a right to be admitted. We understand the Republicans to hold, (and rightly we think,) that, in the words of
their chief organ, the New York *Tribune,* "the admission of a
new State is within the discretion of Congress, and cannot be
claimed as a right;" nor are we aware of any act of the party or
its representatives in Congress, which conflicts with this doctrine, or implies a denial of the right of Congress to say there
shall be no more Slave States in the Union. The attempt was
a dishonest one, to make their action in the last Congress seem
to favor the new heresies of the sham Democracy on the Slave
question.

The President next rejoiced over the change within Kansas;
falsely ascribing it to those proceedings of Congress which he
had so falsely interpreted. "The pressure of external influence," which had caused so much trouble there, was alluded to
in such a way as would lead a reader, ignorant of the facts, to
suppose that the evil influence came from the opposers of his
policy; whereas he knew very well that it came from his own
staunch supporters, who began their work of violence and fraud
before the Territory was organized; and continued it with unre-
lenting pertinacity, aided and encouraged too by the General

Government and its official underlings, until the growing strength of the Free State party fairly overbore and vanquished them. "Resistance to the Territorial Government," said the President, "has been finally abandoned." Yes, and because — which he did not say — the men whom he slanderously accused of "resistance to rightful authority," had wrested it after a severe and protracted struggle against Pro-Slavery usurpation, backed by Executive favor and patronage, from the hands of Border Ruffians and Buchanan Democrats; and had made it to represent the majority of the people of Kansas. "The experience of Kansas," continues the sage moralizer of the White House, "has enforced the lesson that resistance to lawful authority, under our form of government, cannot fail in the end to prove disastrous to its authors." A sort of Balaam's curse, this; turned into a blessing in spite of the utterer's maledictive intent. For it amounts to an unmeant confession that the real "authors of resistance to lawful authority" were the now utterly defeated and dispersed Pro-Slavery party; and not the maligned Free State men, now victors over the combined force of their adversaries, and acknowledged masters of the Territory. It is to the former, not the latter, that this strife has proved "disastrous in the end."

That the President should speak of the fraudulent Lecompton Convention, as legitimately representing the people of Kansas — who, he knew, had reprobated it with the strongest emphasis by an overwhelming majority — and of the Constitution framed by it, as "unexceptionable in its general features," though he knew it was a cunning device to insure the triumph of Slavery; that he should reiterate the falsehood that the Slavery question was submitted to the people, though he knew that only a certain clause was submitted, and in such a way as to make every vote upon it a vote *for* the Constitution, other parts of which would establish Slavery, even if that were voted down; that he should calumniously accuse those who would not be caught in this trap, of "preferring that Slavery should continue rather than surrender their revolutionary Topeka organization;" that he should persist in styling the Border Ruffian usurpation a "lawful government," and imputing to its opposers the guilt of "civil strife and rebellion;" that, while prating of "the just equality of all the States," he should heartily accept the proposal to require of Kansas a larger population for admission as a Free than as a Slave State, and at the same time, in recommending the passage of a general law that no State shall hereafter be admitted till its population equals the ratio required for a Representative in Congress, should except Pro-Slavery, Sham-Democratic Oregon, whose population is less than that of Kansas; all this, and much more of kindred character, contained in the Message, was to have been expected from that quarter, as a matter of course. A decent show of truth and fairness, to say nothing of a genuine sympathy with Freedom and right, would have been too much to ask of the animate "Platform" of a party long ago sold to work wickedness for the behoof of Slavery.

The Message elicited some discussion in Congress, in which its misrepresentations of Kansas matters were sharply criticised; but the session passed without any legislation particularly relating to Kansas.

OREGON.

A bill to admit Oregon into the Union, which had passed the Senate a year before, was reported to the House of Representatives on the 10th of February, and debated till the afternoon of the 12th, when it passed by a vote of 114 to 103. It was vigorously opposed on several grounds, but chiefly on these two: that if the rule as to population was to be insisted on in the case of Kansas, it ought also to be in that of Oregon; and that the proposed Constitution of Oregon is Anti-Republican and conflicts with the Federal Constitution, in forbidding free colored persons to live in the State, or sue in its Courts, thus denying the "privileges and immunities of citizens" there, to a portion of the citizens of some of the other States.

The Washington correspondent of the *Anti-Slavery Standard*, referring to the debate on the 11th, says :—"It was apparent that day that there are Republicans in Congress who hate Slavery, and do not share in the wicked and disgraceful prejudice against color which exists in every State of this Union." He adds that DAWES, of Massachusetts, C. B. COCHRANE, of New York, and BINGHAM, of Ohio, made "the three great speeches of the day," all of them being "principally upon the anti-negro features of the Oregon Constitution." The first ably defended "that class of Massachusetts citizens insulted and struck down by that document," and exposed the inconsistency and refuted the sophistry of his colleagues, COMINS and THAYER, who spoke and voted for the bill. "BINGHAM's speech was a stream of burning eloquence in defence of the rights of the colored man, and he was listened to by every man in the House; and perhaps the most attentive listeners were the Slaveholders present." He denounced the provisions against the colored people, as violating not only the Federal Constitution, but the law of nature; declared that, by the public law of the civilized world, every free man is entitled to live in the land of his birth; that Oregon, by admission into the Union, becomes part of the country of every American citizen; that no State has a right to exile its native freemen, or deny them a fair hearing in its courts of justice; that "not to legalize this horrid injustice was America allowed to assume her proud place among the nations; not to this end the fathers of the Republic put forth their great Declaration, and defended it through a seven years' war, and, with the blood of Yorktown yet fresh upon their garments, proclaimed to the world, and asked it to be held in everlasting remembrance, 'that the rights for which America had contended, were the rights of human nature.'"

The same writer characterizes the speech of ELI THAYER as "cold-blooded, monstrous, and disgraceful;" as apologizing "for those villanous negro-haters in the Free States, who have put upon their statute-books laws which would crimson the cheek of the worst despot in Europe;" and as thus "misrepresenting his constituents," the people of "good old Worcester County, the heart of Massachusetts."

With the great body of the Sham Democracy, a portion of the Republican members must share the deep disgrace of having, by the admission of Oregon, given countenance, and, so far as an act of Congress could, validity to the Anti-Republican, unjust, and basely cruel provision of the Oregon Constitution, which outlaws the colored race, in defiance alike of the principles of public law the world over, and of that eternal right ordained of God to be the universal law; and even in violation of what a certain class of politicians seem to think of still higher authority,

3

the Constitution of the United States. Of the eighty-eight Republican members who voted on the question, fifteen (including two from Massachusetts,) voted in favor of admission, as did also seven of the seventeen Anti-Lecompton Democrats present. Had these, or even but six of them, voted the other way, Oregon would have been told to wait till she had shown regard enough for justice and true Democracy to expunge the gross iniquities of her Constitution, before she could come into the Union.

While the bill was before the House, GROW, of Pennsylvania, moved a substitute, defining the boundaries of Oregon and Kansas, and authorizing the legal voters resident in each Territory, to take the necessary steps for establishing a State Government, their Constitutions to be subject to the approval of the people; but the Speaker ruled it out, as not in order. In the same way he disposed of an amendment which GROW then offered, to repeal the prohibitory clause in the Kansas Compromise Bill. DAVIS, of Indiana, then moved to recommit the bill, with instructions to the Committee to add another section repealing the prohibitory clause of the Kansas bill, and providing that Oregon shall not be admitted, until it has been ascertained by a census that the population is enough for one representative in Congress. The Speaker decided the motion to be out of order, and, on appeal, the House sustained the decision by 118 to 95; thus insisting, in effect, that Kansas, because of her hostility to the designs of the Slave Power, shall still be subject to restrictions from which Pro-Slavery Oregon, ruled by the vassals of that Despotism, shall be exempt. Yet, after this, as we have seen, Republicans enough for the purpose could be found, to turn the doubtful scale in favor of the consummation of this wrong and insult, by admitting Oregon with her atrocious Constitution. Should it be said, as an excuse for them, that Oregon is a Free State, and her admission will strengthen the cause of Freedom in the Union, our answer is a repetition of what we said a year ago, that so far as her relation to the great issue before the country goes, she is free in name alone, and is practically an ally of the oppressor; in the words of the *New York Tribune*, "as thorough and servile a satrapy of the Slave Power as Arkansas."

CUBA.

To acquire Cuba has been, from the first, one of the cherished purposes of BUCHANAN's Administration, as, for years before his inauguration, it was of the master he serves. The past year has witnessed some movements on his part, and that of his partizans in Congress, aiming at the achievement of this purpose; but thus far with no perceptible success.

The President, in his Annual Message, brought the subject before Congress, in connection with complaints of the "unsatisfactory condition" of "our relations with Spain;" of grievances suffered at the hands of Spanish officials in Cuba; and of the difficulty of obtaining redress, because the Captain-General is not empowered to grant it, and the claims for it must be presented "through our minister at Madrid." "The truth is," said he, "that Cuba, in its existing colonial condition, is a constant source of injury and annoyance to the American people;" whence he would evidently have them infer that they ought, with all convenient speed, to put an end to this annoying "colonial condition," by getting the island into their own possession; after which, the cutting of it up into two or three Slave States is expected soon to follow, as a matter of course. Moreover, there is a philanthropic, as well as a patriotic, motive for the President's anxiety to appropriate the coveted prize. His righteous soul and tender heart are deeply grieved by the participation of Cuba in the *African* Slave Trade. "It is the only spot in the civilized world, where the African Slave Trade is tolerated. * * * * * As long as this market shall remain open, there can be no hope for the civilization of benighted Africa. While the demand for Slaves continues in Cuba, wars will be waged among the petty and barbarous chiefs in Africa, for the purpose of seizing subjects to supply this trade. In such a condition of affairs, it is impossible that the light of civilization and religion can ever penetrate these dark abodes." But if Cuba were annexed to this country, "the last relic of the African Slave Trade would instantly disappear." So then, that "the light of civilization and religion" may some day find access to "benighted Africa," Cuba must come into the American Union, and buy her Slaves thenceforward from

Virginia and Maryland, instead of Congo; unless, indeed, her coming in should turn the trembling scale in favor of the reöpening of the trade in men between Africa and this country, and thus not only keep the Cuban market open, but add thereto the vastly more extensive one of all the Slave-consuming region of this continent. This, should it happen, would only *change*, as we may be allowed to hope, the Presidential reasons for rejoicing in the glorious event, and it might then be cause of " gratitude to the Almighty Providence," not that a market for Slaves from Africa is closed, but that a wider sphere of beneficent activity is given to that grand missionary agency, whereby the heathen and barbarian tribes are brought within the full meridian splendor of " the light of civilization and religion," instead of being left to wait for its scattered rays " to penetrate their dark abodes."

Again recurring to patriotic considerations, the President reminded Congress that " the island of Cuba, from its geographical position, commands the mouth of the Mississippi, and the immense and annually increasing trade, foreign and coastwise, from the valley of that noble river, now embracing half the sovereign States of the Union. With that island under the dominion of a distant foreign power, this trade, of vital importance to these States, is exposed to the danger of being destroyed in time of war, and it has hitherto been subjected to perpetual injury and annoyance in time of peace. Our relations with Spain, which ought to be of the most friendly character, must always be placed in jeopardy while the existing Colonial Government over the island shall remain in its present condition."

Having thus made it plain beyond a doubt that "the possession of the island would be of vast importance to the United States," it only remained to show — i. e., to *affirm* — by way of completely clinching the argument, that "its value to Spain is comparatively unimportant." That done, the whole case is made out conclusively; for what right had Spain any longer to demur to the surrender of what is to her such a mere trifle, and to this country is worth so much? What, against reasoning so conclusive, are those paltry grounds of refusal, "it is mine," "I am the proper judge of its value to me," and "it is for me to say whether I will sell it at any price?" Was ever pirate or highwayman turned back from the seizure of his prey by such trivial considerations? And are not the rights of this great and powerful nation, in relation to its weaker neighbors, as ample as the pirate's and highwayman's toward unarmed wayfarers by sea or land? Of course, as the President very properly said, Cuba is to be acquired "by honorable negotiation. We would not, if we could, acquire it in any other manner." But a key to the possible meaning of "honorable negotiation" is furnished in the significant allusion, immediately following, to the acquisition of territory from Mexico "by fair purchase;" for everybody knows how that "fair purchase" was achieved, with the price persuasively tendered on the bayonets of a conquering army. And if this hint were not enough, the lack was fully supplied, (so at least Spain thought,) by the implications of the closing sentence in the next paragraph, wherein the President declared that "this course [of honorable negotiation] we shall ever pursue, *unless* circumstances should occur, which we do not now anticipate, *rendering a departure from it clearly justifiable,* under the imperative and overruling law of self-preservation." To those who know just how much is included in a Pro-Slavery American politician's notion of "self-preservation," this language needs no interpreter.

After intimating that a "large appropriation may be required to effect the purpose" of the contemplated negotiation, and that "it may become indispensable to success that" he "should be entrusted with the means of making an advance to the Spanish Government immediately after the signing of the treaty, without awaiting the ratification of it by the Senate," the President concluded by "commending the whole subject to the careful consideration of Congress."

If ever grave, official document displayed a cooler impudence than this — the circumstances all considered — it has not been our lot to meet the instance. So often and emphatically has Spain avowed her settled purpose never to sell Cuba at any price, nor even to listen to proposals for the purchase of it, that she has reason to regard as little short of a deliberate insult, the pertinacious pressing of negotiation professedly for that object. It is, moreover, as foolish as indecent, if friendly bargaining alone is really meant, and not the seeking of some pretext for a quarrel, to end in taking forcible possession of the island, as "indemnity for the past and security for the future;" while, if the latter is the real intention, its wickedness outgoes its folly.

How the people of Cuba viewed it, we have their own decisive testimony. When the Message was received there, the Corporation of Havana promptly adopted an Address to the Queen of Spain, which "was signed by the Governor of the city, all the officials, and the great body of the citizens." In it they say, they have "not read without profound surprise the recent Message of the President of the United States, in which the infamous idea is announced that that Government has intended, and intends to purchase the island of Cuba, a pretension which must be looked upon as doubly insulting to the nobleness of the nation and to the dignity of the sons of Cuba, who, it appears, are considered no better than a drove of Slaves, that can be sold like a private estate. * * * * * The shame of being sold cannot be supported by those who always appreciate their existence as a part of a nation to which they have ever been assimilated in habit, religion, and customs, and which transmitted to them the beautiful language of Cervantes. The Government of Spain has not heard, and doubtless will not listen to, an ignominious pretension which wounds its sense of decency, but nevertheless the first municipality of the island has believed it to be its duty to raise its voice to your Majesty, on seeing written this insult to humanity and the enlightened age in which we live." They speak of the "cool contumely and total forgetfulness of all the admitted principles of international relations" exhibited in the Message; refer to the refusal of the city, when occupied by the English, in the last century, to do homage to the king of England; and add that "Cuba is the same Spanish province that it has been heretofore. Now and ever it will reject foreign domination."

No less emphatic was the tone of the Cuban press. The *Prensa de la Habana* said "it is hardly necessary for us to remark that the above memorial is the genuine and unanimous expression of the feelings of all the population of Cuba." The *Diario de la Marina* "called the attention of the world to the contrast between our national spirit and American greed; and in what manner the chivalrous temper of our people responds to the mercantile cupidity of American politics, which has prompted the words of the last Presidential Message rela-

tive to this island;" and adds that "such forgetfulness of social
proprieties" as appears in the Message, "intermixed with such
reckless doctrines in regard to the rights of nations, may not
amaze the world, simply because it is accustomed to such aber-
rations on the part of the Washington Cabinet." "Purchase
the island of Cuba!" it exclaimed. "The Washington Cabinet well knows it cannot be bought; that the United States
have not the money which could buy it. Such is the opinion of
all Spaniards, such has been especially the opinion of the natives of the soil, from the first moment the project figured in
the politics of the North. When a minister of the Crown, on
an occasion similar to that produced by the present Message,
said, that to sell the island of Cuba would be to sell the honor
of Spain, the words were reëchoed by the unanimous voice of
the Spanish race, and have been adopted from that moment as
the neatest and most concise formula of reply whenever this
absurd project should be revived. * * * * * The mere enun-
ciation of this design is, for our race, the grossest of insults."
After alluding to the wealth of the island, its commerce, its
advantageous site and material excellences, the *Diario* continued
thus: "But these considerations do not enter into the thoughts
of our people, our sovereigns, our governors, even the humblest
of our countrymen, when they debate this proposed purchase,
which they regard as an insult, and this sale which they regard
as infamy. It is because they have regard to the Spaniards
born in Cuba, brethren of those born in the peninsula, sharers
in the same glory, trained in the same civilization, the same
faith, and the same customs. It is this blood which is price-
less — this civilization which cannot be sold."

The response of Spain, to the Message, was quite as explicit
and decided as that of Cuba. On the 31st of December the
subject was introduced into the lower House of the Spanish
Cortes, by Señor ULLOA, Director General of the Colonies;
and was discussed by some of the most distinguished members
of that body, with a calm dignity and grave earnestness as well
befitting the publicly recognized defenders of a nation's rights
and honor, as the bluster and bombast of our American apostles of "Manifest Destiny" suits the part they have chosen to
enact.

"I am about," said Señor ULLOA, "to occupy the Cortes with

one of those questions which always arouse a unanimous feeling in a noble and generous people like our own; one of those questions which, when put, are always instantly answered, because there is, because there can be, but one answer for them." Alluding to the President's Message he said, it "contains a blunder offensive to the Spanish nation, a continued and concerted offence, to which the Spanish nation ought to reply with dignity and energy through its legitimate representatives." Then, — with a hint that the real object of the President was only "to revive dead hopes, as a foundation for a wished for reëlection," (how should they know in Spain the secret springs of American statesmanship?) with a glance at the demand, constantly repeated by the United States, that the Captain-General of Cuba should be invested with full power to treat on international affairs, which is the exclusive prerogative of the Supreme Government;" and with a trenchant side stroke, in passing, at "those philanthropic pretensions put forth in that discourse in favor of the African race, which indeed, are strange enough, coming as they do from a country where there are States in which Slavery is preserved in its most repugnant form, where this unhappy race is treated like a race of brutes, and where the most atrocious penalties are imposed, not only upon those who have committed the crime of getting a little instruction, but also who are caught in the fulfilment of their religious duties"—he proceeded to cite and comment on the more gravely offensive portion of the Message. Quoting a paragraph or two in full, he said, "here the question of the purchase of Cuba by the United States is put in a very clear manner, and this pressing it after the refusals which have been given to former purchasers, I believe to involve an offence to Spanish honor and dignity. * * * * * It concerns a negotiation which is impossible. In saying so, I speak the general sentiments of the country. * * * * * We are not poor enough to have to live upon the price of this sale; but were we much poorer than we are, Spain would never have recourse to such means to get out of her difficulties. This mercantile policy, in the least noble sense of the word, which the President of the United States has adopted with so much enthusiasm, will forever encounter in Spain a feeling of repulsion which is fostered by the Castilian nobility. This must be known once for all.

But such is the eagerness of the President and the party he represents, that, presuming upon the end which these strange negotiations must have, he enters into the mysteries of the future, and presents us a menace in the distance." Then, repeating the sentence above cited, which contemplates something beside negotiation as possible "under the law of self-preservation," the speaker continued: "this language is sufficiently explicit; the idea is involved in none of those diplomatic nebulosities which are generally used in this class of documents. I am glad of it, and I believe that this House and all Spain will join with me in this for two reasons; first, because civilized Europe shall by this know what are the intentions of a political party of the United States, which is powerful enough to raise its chiefs to the supreme magistracy, and shall also appreciate to the full the new principle of the law of nations, which, according to the happy phrase of a French paper, consists in 'proclaiming the right of forcible appropriation for cause of American utility;' and secondly, because when these intentions are known, her Majesty's Government and the whole nation will prepare against the contingency with which we are threatened, and when these circumstances which Mr. BUCHANAN speaks of shall come, the Spanish nation may reply, as did the Greek hero: 'You want Cuba; then come and take her.'" He concluded by asking the Government and all parties in the House to unite in "a solemn declaration which shall put a stopper upon this threat, this offence; and, whatever may be contained in similar demonstrations which may be made."

He was followed by the Minister of State, who was "glad" of the opportunity "to explain the opinion of her Majesty's Government upon the document" referred to. "I could but be surprised," said he, "that this document should say our relations are in an unsatisfactory state. * * * * * I was profoundly convinced that the relations between the two Governments were perfectly friendly, and ran no risk of disturbance. Her Majesty's Government has still this confidence." After reciting some of the negotiations between the two countries, to justify this statement, and referring to the past history of Spain, he added, "as it is not possible that the Spanish nation should resign any territory which constituted a part of the once vast domains of the Spanish monarchy, the present Government

4

regards it as a duty to make a solemn declaration, which cannot fail to engrave itself on the heart of the Cortes, and to be transmitted to every Spaniard. To-day, to-morrow, on whatever occasion, prosperous or adverse, * * * * * the Spanish nation will never be insensible to its honor, will never dispossess itself of the least part of its territory; and any proposition made with that object will be considered by the Government as an insult offered to the nation."

This speech was applauded long and loudly. Then Señor OLOZAGA, leader of the opposition, and formerly Prime Minister, moved a resolution "that the Cortes has heard with the greatest satisfaction the explanations given by the Government, and that it adheres to the sentiment of those explanations, and is ready to give its constant support to the preservation of the integrity of the Spanish dominions."

In his speech supporting the resolution, he said, "when we all share the desire, which the Government has just expressed, to repel everything offensive to the nobleness and dignity of the Spanish nation, it is just that we should all protest against the tendencies of this insult which is offered to us. * * * * * It would be improper for me to delay the moment which you all desire, of showing that there are no parties in Spain, nor any difference of opinion among Spaniards, upon the question of the conservation of dignity and honor, which is of more account than all the interests of the world. I hope that the House will approve of this proposition, in the interest of the national dignity, in the interest of the Island of Cuba, whose religion, whose customs, whose laws, whose traditions, whose existence, whose future, absolutely depend on the preservation of Union with the mother country, and also in the interest of this very American nation, which we cannot fail to admire and to love, provided that it does not invade, but respect, the just rights of others, in order that a precedent so fatal to the public law of nations may not be admitted."

The resolution was unanimously adopted.

On the 4th of January, the upper House of the Cortes took up the subject and unanimously resolved, "That the Senate tenders to her Majesty's Government its entire support and most efficacious coöperation in every contingency, in view of the Message which has just been delivered by the President of the

United States, and that the Senate is convinced that the national honor and the integrity of the territory of Spain and her transatlantic provinces will come out of this new ordeal unscathed."

The Minister of State, in speaking on the resolutions, said that during his Ministry, there had been no indication referring to the acquisition of Cuba, and if any such should be made to him as Minister of Spain, by a representative of any foreign power, he would "hasten to interrupt him as soon as his intentions were understood, and would tell him what his insinuations were causing in the minds of all Spaniards."

In the United States Senate, Mr. SLIDELL, of Louisiana, on the 10th of January, introduced a bill for placing $30,000,000 in the President's hands "to facilitate the acquisition of Cuba by negotiation." It was referred to the Committee on Foreign Affairs, from which, on the 24th, Mr. SLIDELL presented a long report in favor of the bill; and Mr. SEWARD, a minority report, calling on the President for information, to be transmitted to Congress, at the next session, to enable it to judge whether extraordinary measures are necessary to maintain the country's rights and interests in regard to Spain. An able discussion ensued, but no action was then taken. On the 25th of February, SLIDELL announced the purpose of the majority to force the bill to a final vote before adjournment; but was met with a resolute resistance, which, after the sitting had been protracted by speeches, motions to adjourn, and various "dilatory motions," till one o'clock at night, at last prevailed, and the Senate adjourned. The next day SLIDELL abandoned the bill, despairing of his ability to force it through in the brief remnant of the session.

The piratical party, however, as is evident from the tone of its press, and the speeches of its orators, by no means intends to consider this defeat decisive of the fate of its cherished scheme. "Cuba must and shall be ours," said Senator BROWN, of Mississippi, in a speech made in New York city, on the 14th of last March. "The decree has gone forth, and nowhere on earth is there power to remove it. The only question for us to consider is this: by what means shall we make the acquisition? Three modes have been proposed: purchase, that I regard as the most honorable; conquest, and that I regard as the most certain; and the mysterious operation known as filibusterism, and that I regard as the most probable; but, by one or the other, or all combined, Cuba must and shall be ours. If Spain is disposed to sell the island, I, for one, stand prepared to pay for it. If Spain be indisposed to sell, I would seize Cuba as indemnity for the past, and then negotiate for future security. If BUCHANAN and CASS can't be brought to that point, I would repeal the [neutrality] laws, and cry 'speed to the filibuster, and let slip the dogs of war.' I have grown weary of having young, proud, glorious America knocking at the door of Spain and asking for admission. * * * * * It may be asked, what do we want of Cuba? We want it for territorial expansion. 'Let no pent up Utica contract our powers; the whole boundless universe shall be ours.' * * * * * Then we want it for national defence. The island blocks up the Mississippi, with all its products. We want it to extend our agricultural resources; to get more and cheaper sugar. We want it to extend our commerce. Then, I have a little private reason of my own. I want Cuba for the *extension of Slavery.* I speak for myself, and those who agree with me. * * * * * If it were to come in as a free territory, my courage would very much ooze out at the points of my fingers. I am a Pro-Slavery man; I believe that Slavery is of divine origin, that the African race, from their creation, were doomed to be Slaves to the white man." Addressing the reporters, he said: "report me as I have spoken. When I have spoken in favor of Slavery, report me in the first person. I believe I have spoken the sentiments of my own heart, and of a vast majority of the Democracy throughout the Union. The Democratic party are going into the next Presidential canvass upon this (the Cuban) and other questions, and we intend to meet Seward face to face upon it."

Here is at least a sufficiently frank avowal of the principles by which the Senator — and, as he believes, the vast majority of his party — is governed, and would have the nation governed in its intercourse with other nations. A precious specimen of political morality it is, too!— a genuine chapter from the pirate's and highwayman's ethical code. And if we may credit the testimony of one who has been active in enterprises kindred to this for the seizure of Cuba, "General" WALKER, of Nicaraguan notoriety, this sort of morality has adherents in a higher quarter than the Senate chamber, as devoted if not as frank as the Mississippi Senator. True, the character of the witness gives little weight to his testimony; but its intrinsic probability makes it worthy of attention, even from such a source. In a letter to the Mobile *Register*, dated July 19th, 1858, WALKER said that about the middle of the preceding October, while he was in New Orleans, preparing to return to Nicaragua, General HENNINGSEN arrived from Washington, and stated that, in an interview he had held there with the Secretary of War, "the Secretary had informed him of the President's determination to arrest the expedition to Nicaragua; adding, that the acquisition of Cuba during his administration was an object dear to the heart of Mr. BUCHANAN, and if we would enter the Mexican service we should have the support of the United States Government, and while in that service we might by some act, such as tearing down the flag of Spain, bring about a war between Mexico and Spain, and Mexico might then seize Cuba; and that means would not be lacking for such an enterprise. When pressed to tell how the means could be had, the Secretary replied, that before he could say more he must see a person above him. At a later interview he said, he was not authorized to go further, but they might rely implicitly on the means being provided if the enterprise were undertaken." WALKER added, that at his trial in New Orleans, he endeavored to place these facts in the shape of legal evidence, and for that purpose summoned HENNINGSEN as a witness; but when the question was put to elicit the facts, the District Attorney objected, and the presiding Justice ruled it out without waiting to hear for what object it was asked. Whether this is to be regarded as equivalent to confessing that WALKER's charge is true, the public must judge.

THE SOUTHERN REPUBLICS.

If the President is not scheming to take advantage, in Slavery's behalf, of the internal dissensions of Mexico and the weakness of the States of Central and South America, he unfortunately lays himself open to strong suspicion of such design, by his eagerness to get at least the *power* to do mischief in that direction; asking repeatedly, in person and through his partisans in Congress, for authority, in effect, to plunge the country into war with those feeble States at his own single will. In his Annual Message he "earnestly recommended to Congress the passage of an act authorizing the President, under such restrictions as they may deem proper, to employ the land and naval forces of the United States in preventing the transit [across Nicaragua,— also by the Panama and Tehuantepec routes,] from being obstructed by lawless violence, and in protecting the lives and property of American citizens travelling thereon." On the 11th of January, Mr. MASON, of Virginia, introduce ! into the Senate from the Committee on Foreign Relations, a bill in accordance with the President's recommendation, empowering him, whenever, in *his* opinion, the case demands his interposition, to use the land and naval forces of the United States in such way as in *his* judgment may be most effectual, by force to protect or relieve citizens of the United States, in Mexico, Central or South America, from any injury offered or done by "those claiming to be in authority therein;" and requiring him to report to Congress as soon as possible what he may have done under this authority, and to withdraw the forces as soon as the object shall have been attained. As Congress did not hasten to second the Senator's zeal, the President sent in a Special Message, reminding that dilatory body of "the great urgency and importance of legislative action" for the desired purpose, before the close of the session; repeating nearly word for word, his former recommendation; and backing it with the assurance that, without such a law as he asked for, "the President may be placed in a painful position before the meeting of the next Congress." But this pathetic appeal was ineffectual. Congress adjourned without granting his request; thinking, doubtless, that it was better to risk his chance of a "painful position" than to relieve him with a military dictatorship;—an opinion in which the country evidently concurs. For the present, therefore, this ingenious scheme for "extending the area" of the very peculiar sort "of Freedom" known as American, appears to be a failure.

But it is said, whether or not on good authority, certainly with much intrinsic probability, that the Cabinet at Washington is considering another way of turning the distracted condition of Mexico to the advantage of Slavery; that it is discussing a proposal to recognize the so-called "Liberal" Government on condition that the Marshals of the United States shall be permitted to pursue, arrest, and bring back Fugitive Slaves escaping into Mexico. It would be much easier, however, we doubt not, for President BUCHANAN to offer than for President JUAREZ to accept such terms. If the "Liberal" Chief himself were base enough to listen to them, his own followers would desert him. We cannot believe that any party in Mexico, sad as the condition of that country is, has yet sunk low enough to entertain a proposition so disgraceful; and thus the moral certainty of its rejection, if offered — rather than any sense of shame, or regard for right, or respect for Mexican sovereignty on Mexican soil — may prevent the offer.

NEW SLAVE STATES IN PROSPECT.

Meanwhile, the Slave Power is not neglectful of its opportunities within the present boundaries of the Union. To compensate itself for the now almost certain loss of Kansas, it is scheming to divide California, and make a Slave State of the southern portion; while it hastens eagerly to clutch New Mexico, as if that were, beyond controversy or question, its own. On the 5th of March a bill was introduced into the Senate of California, for the division of the State, setting off all south of the thirty-sixth degree of latitude as a separate Territory, which, of course, the Slaveholders mean, as speedily as possible, to appropriate, and erect into a new State. The Territorial Legislature of New Mexico has, within a few weeks, passed an act recognizing Slavery as a legal institution in that Territory, and guarding it with stringent provisions and severe penalties. It does not attempt to *set up* the system, or *confer* legality upon it, but coolly takes for granted that it is already legal and rightful, and needs only protection and regulation. It provides, for murder or other offence upon a Slave's person, the same penalty as if he were free and white; for stealing a Slave, with intent to deprive the master of "the use and benefit" of him,— whether by carrying him away with violence, or by enticing him, with such intent, to go, or for aiding or advising therein, or for conveying or assisting to convey a Slave beyond the control of his master, with intent to aid his escape, or for secreting him from his master,—imprisonment, net more than ten nor less than four years, and a fine of not more than two thousand, nor less than five hundred dollars; for furnishing a Slave with forged free papers, imprisonment not more than five years, nor less than six months, and a fine of not more than a thousand, nor less than a hundred dollars; for inducing a Slave to absent himself from his master's service, or for harboring a Slave so absenting himself, the same penalty, besides liability to a civil suit for damages; for endeavoring to excite in a Slave a spirit of insurrection, or aiding him in resisting his master, or furnishing him any deadly weapon or ammunition, (except temporarily by the master, for the lawful defence of the master's person, family, or property,) or for trading with a Slave, unless he has a written permit from the master specifying the articles he may trade in, or for furnishing to a Slave a forged permit to trade,—imprisonment not less than three months, nor more than three years, and a fine of not less than twenty-five, nor more than a thousand dollars; for playing with a Slave any game of skill or chance, a fine not exceeding a hundred dollars, or imprisonment not exceeding three months, or both, at the Court's discretion.   It provides that any person may take up any runaway Slave, using such force as is necessary, and, if no reward has been offered, shall, on delivery of the Slave to his master, or to the sheriff of the county, be entitled to twenty dollars, besides ten cents a mile for his travel to and from the place of apprehension.   If the sheriff refuse to receive and keep the runaway, he shall be fined not less than five hundred dollars, be liable to the owner for the Slave's value, and be ineligible for reëlection.   He must advertise the runaway six months, unless an owner sooner appears; and if none then appears, must sell him to the highest bidder, after six or seven months' notice of the day of sale, and pay the net proceeds to the Territorial Treasurer.   Any owner failing to maintain his Slave, shall be required to give bond for his support.   The owner of a Slave indicted for felony shall be cited to appear and defend the Slave, and if he fail to do so, the Court is to appoint counsel for the Slave, at the owner's expense. Cruel treatment of a Slave by his owner shall be punished by imprisonment not more than a year, and fine not more than a thousand dollars.   [We may judge the comparative enormity of different offences, from the fact that the highest penalty for cruel treatment is, in imprisonment one-tenth, in fine one-half the *highest*, or in imprisonment one-fourth, in fine double the *lowest* penalty for helping a Slave's escape from bondage.] For suffering a Slave to hire his own time, or employ himself as a freeman for more than twenty-four hours at once, the owner shall be fined not more than one hundred dollars. Disorderly conduct in public, or insolent language or signs to a free white person, by a Slave, shall be punished with stripes on the bare back, not exceeding thirty-nine. Slaves shall be punished with stripes, or branding, for crimes of which the legal penalty is a money-fine. No Slave, or free negro, or mulatto, can testify in any court against a free white person; but they can against each other. Marriages between white persons and Slaves, or free negroes or mulattoes, are forbidden and declared void, and any white person attempting to enter into or procure such marriage, shall be imprisoned not more than six months, and fined not more than five hundred dollars. Emancipation of Slaves is totally prohibited. A Slave found off his master's premises after sunset and before sunrise, without a written pass, may be taken before a justice of the peace by any white person, and shall be whipped not more than thirty-nine stripes on the bare back, and imprisoned till the next day, to be released then on payment of costs by the owner. A claim to the possession of a Slave may be prosecuted by writ of replevin, or by writ of habeas corpus. Any person holding as a Slave a negro or mulatto legally free, shall be imprisoned not more than ten nor less than five years, and be fined not more than two thousand, nor less than five hundred dollars. Such are, in substance, the main provisions of the barbarous Slave Code, just enacted by Democratic despotism, in a Territory from which distinguished politicians used to tell us that the laws of climate and physical geography had effectually excluded Slavery.

On the borders of the Western Slave States are four tribes of Indians,—Cherokees, Choctaws, Chickasaws, and Creeks,—so far advanced in civilization, as to be little, if at all, behind their white neighbors. They have regular governments formed by themselves, substantially like those of the adjacent States; and under the fostering care of the Federal Government, and the religious teaching of Missionaries of the American Board, have so diligently developed, and are so sedulously guarding, the

5

"patriarchal institution," that the Slaveholders in the States are beginning to think them worthy of full political fellowship. Their admission into the Union is already suggested, and it is by no means improbable that it will, ere long, be accomplished; the eager desire of the Slave Power to secure so important an accession of political strength being likely to overcome, for the occasion, the Anglo-Saxon spirit of exclusiveness and pride of race. The Southern press begins to argue for the expediency, not to say necessity of such a measure. Says the New Orleans *Picayune*, "The progress of civilization in several of the Indian tribes west of the States, will soon bring up a new question for the decision of Congress. * * * * * . These Indian States cannot exist as independent governments, when the Caucasian race presses upon them. The people, civilized and attached to the soil they have improved, cannot be removed to remoter wilds, nor without serious discontents, is it likely the United States can subject them to the condition of other Territorial organizations, by an abrogation of the Constitutions they have established for themselves;" thus evidently meaning to give the impression that no alternative remains but to admit them to the Union. It adds, significantly, "It cannot fail to give greater interest to this question, that each of these Indian States has adopted the social institutions of the South. The Indians are Slaveholders." It will be less strange than many things which have already happened, if before long Slavery should have eight Senators and four Representatives in Congress from these new Indian States.

NEW DEMAND OF THE SLAVE POWER.

To secure a footing in all the Territories, present and prospective, and to make sure of the whole period of their territorial condition for establishing itself firmly, and gaining power to control their organization as States, the Slave Power is now urging a new demand. Having triumphed in the last Presidential election by means of the pretence of its Northern allies that they were contending for "Popular Sovereignty" and "Congressional non-intervention" in the Territories, it now proposes to make the utmost possible advantage of its victory by repudiating these delusive doctrines, and with characteristic audacity insisting that Congress must interve.e to *protect* Slave property in the Territories, whether against hostile, or in defect of friendly, territorial legislation.

Early last fall the Southern press broke ground for this advanced position. The Richmond (Va.) *Enquirer* complains that "t.ie p:.-ent state of Federal legislation is entirely inadequate for the t':.rough and effectual protection of Slave property in the Terr'to)es." Assuming that under the Dred Scott decision "Sla.er, ca..no.: be *prohibited* in a Territory," it asks, "but how can it be *prote.. l?*" and adds, "the general regulations of the Federal code, embracing every species of property, are altogether inadequate for the security of Slave property. Slavery, peculiar in its nature, requires a peculiar adaptation of municipal law for its healthy maintenance. * * * * * The Constitution requires that Slave property shall be protected in the Territories, and it is the business of Congress to furnish this protection directly and immediately. * * * * * *Congress must intervene to protect Slavery in the Territories.* Let us put our shoulder to the wheel, and labor earnestly, faithfully, and prudently for the consummation of this constitutional necessity." And again: " *There must be positive legislative enactment ; a civil and criminal code for the protection of Slave property in the Territories ought to be provided.*" Meanwhile, till this is done, it says, "much, if not all, must depend on the loyalty and efficiency of the President. He appoints the Territorial Executive and Judiciary. It will be the province of this Judiciary to protect Slave property, as far as possible, under the laws of the Federal code for the protection of property generally, and it will be the business of the Territorial Executive to uphold and enforce the authority of the Judiciary. It will be the duty of the President to hold both to a zealous performance of their several offices. Hence, *the next Democratic nominee for the Presidency should be pledged to the protection of Slave property in all the Territories.*" The Charleston (S. C.) *News,* after affirming that "according to the Kansas-Nebraska bill,·and the Dred Scott decision, the Constitution confers upon Slavery the right to go" to the Territories, continues, that "it also imposes the duty of protecting that right, and this cannot be done without positive Pro-Slavery legislation, and A FEDERAL

SLAVE CODE FOR THE TERRITORIES." The Washington *Union* quotes approvingly the Richmond *Enquirer's* declaration that "Virginia holds that Congress has the right, and is in duty bound, to protect Slavery in the Territories, until the people of a Territory, when on the eve of forming a State government, may decide the question finally for the future State. * * * * * This question will have to be met, and the South will demand her constitutional rights, and will demand the legislation necessary to render valid the rights so amply recognized by the [Democratic] party, the country, Congress, the Supreme Court, and the Constitution. * * * * * There is no power to coërce a Territorial Legislature to do its constitutional duty, and Congress *must supply the legislation withheld* by the derelict Territory." Nor is it in the South only that this monstrous doctrine finds advocates. The New York *Day-Book*, one of the most zealous organs of the Sham Democracy, says that "if the people of a Territory, *while they are a Territory*, fail to protect property invested in the person of a negro, they grossly violate equal rights, (!!!) and therefore are *not authorized to consider themselves Democrats.* The whole question is resolved into this simple right or no right to protection to Slave property in the Federal Territories, and as the Charleston *News* suggests, *it must constitute the issue of* 1860." The question was debated at much length in the United States Senate, during the last week of February, and at least two Northern Senators; GWIN, of California, and BIGLER, of Pennsylvania, went with almost the whole body from the South, for Congressional protection to Slavery in the Territories.

This is all which it is thought expedient to demand just now; though it is hard to see why, on any legal or moral ground, the claim should stop here, if the arguments used to urge it so far are sound. If Slaves are property, by the Constitution, what right has a *State*, more than a Territory, to infringe the constitutional right to hold them as such? And he has read to little purpose — if at all — the history of the steady progress of the Slave Power, from aggression to aggression, from encroachment to encroachment, who believes that it *will* stop here, if its present claim is conceded. The next demand will most likely be, that the Federal Government shall protect Slavery in every State into which any Slaveholder may choose to carry it. As an entering wedge for that demand, it is now pressing its claim for such a decision of the well-known LEMMON case as will affirm the right to hold Slaves in transit across any State, Slave or Free; confidently expecting, and not without reason, that, as soon as the case can be brought before the Supreme Court of the United States, the Slaveholding and Pro-Slavery judges who control that tribunal, will promptly give the desired decision. But to reach that point, the case has yet to go through the New York State Court of Appeals, which shows no disposition to hasten its progress. About the middle of last June it came up in that Court, on application of the Slaveholder's counsel, for the hearing of it as a preferred cause. The Court held, however, that it was not entitled to be heard out of its order on the calendar; thinking probably that in no event could harm come of its waiting its turn; since if the decision of the Court below, which had done substantial justice in the matter, is to be finally confirmed, doing it earlier or later will make no material difference; but if it is to be reversed, the later such a triumph of *injustice* is achieved, the better. The case has therefore to take its regular course, and is not expected to be heard in the highest State Court before next year.

THE FOREIGN SLAVE TRADE.

While diligently striving to enlarge its fields, the Slave Power is mindful also of its need of a corresponding increase in the number of its human working tools. The reöpening of the African Slave Trade, in order to meet this want, continues to be urged at the South, and seems to be growing in favor with the people of what may be called the Slave consuming States.

The Southern Commercial Convention, which closed its session at Montgomery (Ala.) on the 14th of last May, spent much of its time in discussing the subject. Two reports laid before it,— one by Mr. SPRATT, of South Carolina, proposing a revival of the Slave Trade, the other by Mr. YANCEY, of Alabama, merely advocating the repeal of all laws which forbid it,— were ordered to be printed, and the whole matter was reserved to be considered by the next Convention, to be held at Vicksburgh, (Miss.) in May, 1859. As so pious a work ought not to lack a religious sanction, a writer in the Vicksburgh *True Southron* proposes that "the Convention raise a fund to be dispensed in premiums for the best sermons in favor of reöpening the African Slave Trade." By all means! The Southern pulpit having already demonstrated to the abundant satisfaction of its hearers, that the system which robs millions at home of man-hood and all its rights is a divine institution, a blessing to the robber and the robbed, the country and the world, let it be encouraged to go on to the legitimate conclusion of its prem-ises, and prove from reason and revelation that the piracy which prowls upon the seas, to pander to the robbery which plunders upon land, is equally beneficent and laudable therewith; a compendious practice of all the virtues; at once patriotic, philanthropic, and Christian; enriching our own country with labor which costs little purchase money at first, and no wages afterward; bestowing on the poor barbarians the benign and civilizing influence of hard work and coarse fare, the lash and the branding iron; and propagating the gospel, not by sending missionaries and bibles to the heathen, but by bringing the heathen from a land without the bible to a country which has it, but forbids their learning to read it. Let it be shown that gain is godliness, and that they who seek first to grow rich by the profits of man-stealing, shall have the kingdom of God and His righteousness added unto them. If the task is somewhat difficult, let the offered reward be proportionately liberal, and no doubt there will be enough of eager competition for it.

To show which way the current of feeling on this subject is setting at the South, the *Southern Citizen* last fall exultingly announced that " JOHN J. MCRAE has been triumphantly elected to Congress from Mississippi,— has even to a wonderful extent harmonized parties, and all by his straightforward advocacy of the Slave Trade with Africa. In one county, where the people were almost all his political opponents, he had nearly every vote." A Charleston correspondent of the same paper says that "in South Carolina, Mr. SPRATT" — mentioned above as advo-cating the revival of the African Slave Trade — "has been elected to the State Legislature by a very large majority; and Mr. PETTIGREW," author of a minority report to the preceding Legislature, opposing that measure, "has failed of his election." The *Citizen* adds, "this cause of 'the traffic in human flesh' advances, and will advance." We learn also from the *South Carolinian*, a leading organ of the ruling party in the State, that before the election the candidates for the Legislature were asked — among other questions designed to test their allegiance to Slavery — "Are you in favor of reöpening the African Slave Trade ? "

De Bow's Review, in its last October number, has even the effrontery to recommend not only "the opening of the Slave Trade," but also, in connection therewith, "the introduction of our peculiar institution into the Western States and Territories," as "the most effectual means of giving perpetuity" to the Union. "By this," it continues, "we will construct a homogeneous system of labor, and thus that community of sentiment will be reëstablished, without which the Constitution is a rope of sand, and the Union a shallow mockery."

A correspondent of the New York *Times*, writing from the South, in November last, speaks of being informed "that a League exists in the Southern States, one of whose aims is to augment the supply of negro labor in the planting States;" and that it claims for the States "a perfect right to legalize and regulate an African Free Apprentice system," which "Congress has no power to prohibit." It is now "operating upon the State of Mississippi, to secure the enactment of a law under which to carry out immediately a system of African apprenticeship, or 'the Slave Trade in disguise.'" Early last summer a firm in Charleston, (S. C.) applied for a clearance to a vessel bound for the coast of Africa, "for the purpose of taking on board African emigrants, in accordance with the United States Passenger Law, and of returning with the same to some port in the United States;" and proposed, in writing, that if the clearance should be granted and the vessel be thus protected in taking in her cargo on the African coast, the landing should be at New Orleans, for the express purpose of testing, before the Courts of the United States, the legality of the proceeding. The Collector of the port referred the application to the Secretary of the Treasury, who refused to sanction it, on the ground that to bring in Africans to be held as Slaves is forbidden by Congress; and to bring them as Freemen is forbidden by all the Slave States and some of the Free, and is desired by none. This refusal was sharply criticised in the Charleston papers, by a Mr.

LAMAR, who stoutly affirmed that the ship was entitled to the clearance asked for, and that the Secretary had no right to presume an intent to violate the law.

The Constitution of Georgia, adopted in 1791, before the manifold excellences of Slavery were discovered, forbids the importation of Slaves into that State "from Africa or any other foreign place." Early last winter a bill was brought into the Legislature, to provide for the striking out of this prohibition, and was defeated by a majority of only one — 47 to 46. In urging its passage, a Mr. ATKINSON argued that, "if we [of the South] first purge our Constitutions and laws of these *Abolition heresies*, we can then consistently ask the North to believe with us; but while we acknowledge the evil of Slavery by prohibiting it from our shores, can we expect them to call it anything but sin? * * * * * The fire of fanaticism is coming down upon us; to resist it successfully, we must put on the panoply of law, and arm ourselves at every point. This we cannot do while we acknowledge that the means by which we acquired it ought to be prohibited." Mr. ATKINSON's logic is much better than his morality. There is certainly no escape from the conclusion it leads to, that if the Foreign Slave Trade is wrong, Slaveholding is not right. The title acquired by purchase is only such as the seller has to give; this being utterly invalid, its flaws can be no way mended by any number of transfers. It is, therefore, strictly true that laws against the Slave Trade imply a condemnation of Slavery. And so they were doubtless understood at the time of their enactment, being then regarded as preliminary steps to the abolition of the Slave system itself. Of course, they are sadly out of keeping with that new policy which looks to the perpetuation of the system.

A manifesto, published last winter by the "League of United Southerners of the City and County of Montgomery," (Ala.) calls the abolition of the Foreign Slave Trade a concession to the aggressive demands of Northern fanaticism; and insists on "the necessity of sustaining Slavery not only where its existence is put directly in issue, but where it is remotely concerned." In the Senate of Arkansas, on the 19th of November last, an attempt to instruct the Senators in Congress from that State, and to request the Representatives, to use their influence against the reöpening of the African Slave Trade, was defeated by a vote of 20 to 2. In the Legislature of Louisiana a bill was introduced in the lower House, and referred to the Committee on Federal Relations, declaring that "the Federal Government has no power to prohibit the buying of negro Slaves. by citizens of this State," and that their right to buy such property in *any* market has never been alienated; and authorizing any citizen, or association of citizens, of Louisiana, to purchase Slaves in Africa, Cuba, and Brazil, and bring them to and hold them in the State, subject however to payment of duties on importation, like "other foreign property." The bill was rejected, but nearly one-third of the votes were in its favor. A letter from a resident in Texas, published a few weeks ago in the New York *Express*, says, "I wish the Slave Trade was reöpened. * * * * * It is the very thing that Texas wants. We could use half a million of the black rascals profitably to work to-morrow. * * * * * A few are smuggled in occasionally. Six hundred have been landed on the coast within the last few weeks, and more are on the way." A letter dated "St. Augustine, (Fla.) March 5th, 1859," attests a growing demand for cheap Slaves in Florida, Georgia, and the Carolinas; alludes to rumors of the landing of cargoes of Slaves on the Gulf coast of Florida, and of more coming; speaks of several vessels "known to be engaged in the business;" and adds, that "if the Slave Trade is not in reality reöpened at this time, the indications are that it soon will be." J. R. GIDDINGS, writing from Washington, states that "an ex-member of Congress, lately returned from a tour in Georgia and Alabama, says that the masses of the people in those States are determined to import Slaves, and openly defy the Federal Government to enforce the laws against the Slave Trade." To show the audacity with which these laws are defied, we have it from the Savannah *Georgian*, that last summer the Executive Committee of an Agricultural Society in Georgia, meeting in Savannah, "unanimously resolved to offer a premium of $25 for the best specimen of a live African imported into the United States within the last twelve months, — to be exhibited at the next meeting of the Society." And in the Enterprise (Miss.) *Weekly News*, of April 14th, WILLIAM S. PRICE, Sen., and seventeen others, in a notice, dated April 10th, 1859, announce "to Shipowners and Masters of our Mercantile Marine," that they "will pay three hundred dollars per head for

6

one thousand native Africans, between the ages of fourteen and twenty years, (of sexes equal,) likely, sound, and healthy, to be delivered within twelve months from this date, at some point accessible by land, between Pensacola, Fla., and Galveston, Texas; the contractors giving thirty days' notice as to time and place of delivery;"—or they "will pay fifty dollars extra, if delivered at Enterprise, Clark County, Miss." To prove their trustworthiness, they refer to several mercantile houses in Mobile, Ala. They "profess to be law-abiding citizens," but believe the act unconstitutional "which interdicts the Slave Trade," and "esteem it a duty to extend the privilege of becoming semi-civilized, by the American institution of domestic Slavery, to others of Africa's degraded race."

DANIEL LEE, editor of the *Southern Cultivator*, and Professor of Agricultural Chemistry in the University of Georgia, writing to the Georgia *Constitutionalist*, in February last, refers to "the fact that the South has now nearly *seven hundred thousand square miles* of unimproved land, and mines of vast extent and inestimable value, which require human labor alone to render both exceedingly productive;" affirms that "fully to meet the *mineral* requirements of the South will demand the labor of a million of men in the next twenty years;" and, in view of these facts, thinks it "providential that there is so much unemployed power in human muscles in western Africa," which "may be had at from ten to fifteen dollars as its exists in each person." He wishes the South "to take a million of men and women now worthless in Africa, and make their labor so productive as to cause the now unproductive Southern mines to pay a good interest on a thousand million dollars, and the muscles of these savages to pay a fair interest on a thousand or five hundred dollars each." He estimates that their work, in one year, "will refund the money paid for them and the cost of bringing them" over, and that "they will then be worth, at five hundred dollars a head, five hundred million dollars to the South, as an enduring, everliving, and reproducing industrial power." Moreover, "under the three-fifths representation in Congress, they will give the South six new Representatives," and will create such a demand for farmers, mechanics, professional men, &c. by their labor as miners, as to bring in a million immigrants from Europe to the South, with a gain of "ten more Representatives in Con-

gress." He argues that to extend its improvements already begun, "to consolidate its strength and harmonize all interests,
the South must draw equally on Europe and Africa for living
men and women;" that to admit "all immigrants from Europe"
and none "from the parent land of the negro, is to discriminate
against the labor of the latter without any good reason;" and
that the moral right "to bring negroes from the valley of the
Niger" to till the land, is the same as to bring "Germans from
their fatherland" to do it. Bringing Africans to this country
as Slaves, he calls by the pleasant name of "aiding these feeble
people to vindicate their manhood;" and says "the fulness of
time has arrived when it is practicable to improve at once men
of the type of WASHINGTON, HAMILTON, JEFFERSON, CLINTON,
MARSHALL, and LIVINGSTON, and the most degraded savages,
with great advantage to the world at large. I trace the growing demand for negro muscles, bones, and brains, to the good
providence of God." How beautiful is piety, especially in learned Professors and sagacious Political Economists!

The *National Era*, favorably situated for observing the direction of Southern sentiment, said, about the middle of last March,
"there can be no doubt that the idea of reviving the African
Slave Trade is gaining ground in the South. Some two months
ago we could quote strong articles from ultra Southern journals
against the traffic; but of late we have been sorry to observe in
the same journals an ominous silence upon the subject, while the
advocates of 'free trade in negroes' are earnest and active."
And, we may add, they seem to be largely represented in Congress, judging from the tone of the debates when, several times
last winter, that theme was touched.

Mr. DOWDELL, of Alabama, spoke of "the reöpening of the
Slave Trade," as "a matter properly belonging to the sovereign
States whose industrial policy is to be affected by it;" and
declared the laws "highly offensive in defining" that trade as
"piracy," and in attaching the death penalty to an act not necessarily immoral. Mr. CLAY, of Kentucky, was "opposed to all
these laws on our statute book, in relation to the Slave Trade."
Mr. SEWARD, of Georgia, looked upon them "as mischievous,
wrong, and a violation of the Constitution," and wished them
repealed, "and the matter left to be settled by the States." Mr.
BARKSDALE, of Mississippi, "endorsed the speech" of Mr. SEW-

ARD. Mr. CRAWFORD, of Georgia, said that "unless the war upon Slavery is stopped, fifteen years will witness the trade open for the South and our then Mexican possessions reaching to Guatemala certainly, and probably further south." Mr. MILES, of South Carolina, was "with all his mind and strength" for "sweeping away laws which stamp the people of his section as pirates, and put a stigma on their institutions." Mr. KEITT, of South Carolina, "would repeal the law declaring the Slave Trade piracy, and withdraw our Slave squadron from the coast of Africa." Senator BROWN, of Mississippi, "would repeal the law instantly, as not based on the Constitution;" and both he and Senator MASON, of Virginia, contended that humanity required the keeping of the rescued captives of the Slaver "Echo" in this country as Slaves. Twenty-eight Southern Representatives voted against an appropriation to pay the cost of sending back those captives to their native land, and forty-five (with *one* from Illinois,) against an appropriation for their support and education during one year after their arrival in Africa. While the bill containing it was before the Committee of the whole House, Mr. SEWARD, of Georgia, moved, on the 26th of January, an amendment, repealing all laws against the Slave Trade, and expressly leaving "with each of the States the policy of restricting" that traffic; but the motion was decided to be out of order. On the 23d of December, Mr. HOUSTON, of Alabama, refused the necessary unanimous consent to the submission by Mr. BLAIR, of Missouri, of a resolution instructing the Judiciary Committee "to report a bill more effectually to prevent the Slave Trade under the guise of 'Coolie Trade,' or 'Apprentices,' or 'African Labor Importation Companies,' or in any other guise;" Mr. GARNETT gave a like refusal to Mr. KILGORE, of Indiana, asking leave to offer a resolution calling on the President for any "information received by him in regard to a recent importation of Slaves from Africa into Georgia;" and Mr. SANDIDGE, of Louisiana, introduced a resolution (which was referred to the Committee on Foreign Relations,) to abrogate the article of the Ashburton Treaty, requiring a squadron to be kept on the African coast for the suppression of the Slave Trade. On the 31st of January, Mr. KILGORE moved a suspension of the rules, that he might offer a preamble and resolutions, which refer to recent demands for a revival of the Foreign Slave Trade, recent denunciations of the laws prohibiting it, and recent demonstrations of a purpose to defy and violate them; affirm the power of Congress to forbid the traffic; declare that no legislation can be too thorough, nor any penalty in modern codes too severe against it; that the laws in force against it are founded on the broadest principles of philanthropy and religion, and should not be changed, unless to make them more efficient; that they should be faithfully executed by the Government, and respected by all good citizens; and that the Executive should be sustained and commended for any proper effort to enforce them, and punish those who violate them. The motion — needing two-thirds to carry it — was defeated by 84 nays to 115 yeas. Only five yeas were from the Slave States; three from Maryland, and two from North Carolina and Kentucky. Fifteen nays were from the North.

The demonstrations alluded to, of an intent to violate and defy the laws against the Slave Trade, might well demand legislative notice, whether for their number, or for the unwonted boldness of some of them. To name them all would make the list too long for our space. Not only have American capital, and skill, and enterprise, as heretofore, been largely invested in carrying on the traffic to other countries, but in one instance, certainly, the human cargo has been brought to this; and the arrival, landing, and distribution of it have been paraded by a portion of the Southern press, in ostentatious contempt of the law and its ministers.

· About the first of December last, the yacht Wanderer, (which, after a temporary detention in New York, last June, on suspicion of being destined for the Slave Trade, was released for want of proof satisfactory to the cautious authorities,) came in from the African coast, and landed several hundred Slaves, near Brunswick, Georgia; whence they were speedily distributed in that and other States. The Augusta *Chronicle*, of December 16th, (opposed to the traffic,) says that " about 270 of the cargo are now on a plantation in South Carolina, two or three miles below this city, on the Savannah river, and we suppose will soon be offered for sale. * * * * The success of this enterprise by the owners of the Wanderer establishes the fact that if the Southern people intend to suppress this traffic they must rely upon themselves. The coast of the Slaveholding

States is so extensive that the entire navy of the United States cannot maintain the law inviolable." The Augusta *Despatch* says, "we learn on good authority, that the cargo consisted of 420. * * * * Citizens of our city are probably interested in the enterprise. It is hinted that this is the third cargo landed by the same company, during the last six months. * * * * One of our citizens has bought from the lot, a stout boy, about fourteen years old, for $250." To show "what practical good can result from the agitation of the revival of the Slave Trade, we point to this cargo of sturdy laborers, delivered from the darkness and barbarism of Africa, to be elevated and Christianized on our soil;" and "to the price paid for this son of the jungles, compared with the exorbitant prices paid for less valuable negroes here; and we claim that these results are the beginning of the blessings to flow in upon the South" from that agitation. "This trade may be called piracy, by a false construction of a foolish law, but the day will come when the South will make it the right arm of her legitimate commerce." A writer in the Edgefield (S. C.) *Advertiser* makes "an authorized announcement that the Slaves brought by the Wanderer have been landed in Edgefield District, and most of them are now within its confines. This act has been done by a combination of many of the first families in Georgia and South Carolina, from purely patriotic motives." A correspondent of the New York *Times*, writes from Montgomery, (Ala.) on December 24th, that he has "just seen the negroes brought from Africa by Capt. CORRIE," of the Wanderer. "They are real Congo negroes. They came here from Macon, Ga. * * * * * So far as a successful landing of a cargo of native Africans on our Southern coast can effect that result, the African Slave Trade has actually been reöpened." The Atlanta (Ga.) *Intelligencer* states that "forty negroes said to be direct from Africa," and believed to be part of the Wanderer's cargo, passed through Atlanta by railroad, going West, on the 23d of December. A little later, a despatch from Savannah says that "scores have been transported by railroads and steamers throughout the South." The Vicksburg (Miss.) *Sun* speaks of two of them as "smuggled into Mississippi," and living "on a plantation bordering on the Mississippi Central Railroad, between Canton and Durant." Other papers, in different parts of the South, mention parties of them as having been in their respective neighborhoods. With all this publicity as to where they were, we hear of no earnest effort of the Government to get possession of the captives, and restore them to freedom and home. One of them was "arrested" on the coast, a few days after the landing, but was soon after "abducted" at night from the place where he had been put for safe keeping; no pains having been taken to guard him securely, though the Marshal had been warned of a probable attempt at abduction. Two others were taken in Macon, and sent to Savannah, where they were kept several weeks in jail, and then given up by a Justice of the Peace, to C. A. L. LAMAR, (the openly avowed owner of the Wanderer,) who claimed them as his property, supporting his claim by proof that they had been seen in his possession. This, it seems, is, by Georgia law, presumptive proof of good title to black men. The United States Attorney and the Marshal had notice of the proceedings but declined to interfere, the latter expressly disclaiming any right to detain the Africans. A Deputy Marshal, in Telfair County, arrested thirty-six on their way to Alabama in charge of one or two men, put them in the county jail, and reported to the Marshal, at Savannah, what he had done. The Marshal replied that he "had telegraphed and written to the authorities at Washington, and had received no answer respecting the Africans known to be in the country, and his advice was to turn them loose and let them go on their way." The Deputy did so; the persons from whom they had been taken, resumed the charge of them, and pursued their journey. A few weeks after this, some persons from Worth County, who had assisted in the arrest, having visited Savannah, LAMAR made oath, before a Justice of the Peace, that they had stolen from him certain negroes of the value of at least $2000; whereupon they were arrested and bound over for trial at the October Term of the Worth Superior Court, on a charge of larceny.

We do not hear of even an attempt to secure any of the remaining hundreds of the imported Africans, and the whole cargo seems now to have sunk into the mass of the Slave population and disappeared.

On the first public knowledge of the Wanderer's arrival, three of her crew were arrested, and, after examination, bound over to answer at the next term of the United States District Court, in

Savannah. Six weeks later, the captain surrendered himself to the United States Marshal, in Charleston, S. C., and was held to bail in $5000. Indictments were found against him in Savannah, but warrants for his arrest were refused by the Judge of the South Carolina District, on the ground that, having been bound over to appear in that District, it was there he ought to be indicted. As yet we have heard of no further proceedings in these cases.

The vessel was condemned as a Slaver, and sold at auction, on the 12th of March, but to LAMAR himself, and, it is said, for less than a quarter of its value. He claimed it as his property, unjustly taken from him; and appealed to the crowd not to bid against him. Very few did so; only one, it seems, to any considerable amount; and him he knocked down, amid general applause. It is affirmed that "the Marshal seemed to favor LAMAR, not dwelling an instant" after his last bid. Thus, instead of promptly taking measures to hold him to account for the piracy in which his own repeated public avowals prove him to have been the real principal, the Government restored to him, with a legal title, and at a price little more than nominal, the forfeited instrument of its perpetration; very probably to be used in repeating the crime. He has since, however, been indicted, for aiding and abetting in the Slave Trade, and for having in his possession, and for claiming, Africans recently imported; but, as a Savannah jury will try him, he is in little danger of conviction.

Two parties of the newly imported Africans having been brought to Mobile, Judge CAMPBELL, of the United States Circuit Court for the Southern District of Alabama, took occasion from that fact, in charging the Grand Jury, at Mobile, on the 12th of April, to expound very distinctly the law concerning the Slave Trade; denouncing in emphatic terms the "piratical efforts lately made to make Slaves of Africans, *in despite of the treaties and laws* of the United States;" and "invoking the active and diligent efforts of the Grand Jury to bring the malefactors to justice." We do not yet hear of any remarkably "diligent efforts" to that end. But the news may not have had time to reach us.

The Washington *Union*, commenting on this case of the Wanderer, talks of "the moral turpitude of the crime," calls it "an act of piracy as sordid and wanton as ever disgraced the times of the buccaneers;" but says, "as a mere question of *philanthropy to the negro*, the persons who have recently brought a cargo of Africans from Guinea, and landed them in Georgia, may have done *a beneficial work*." Assuming that the facts show it to have been "in accordance with public opinion" in Georgia, it says, "the Federal tribunals stand a poor chance of honestly executing the laws, in a community who not only wink at the crime committed, but aid the criminal in rendering" it "profitable and safe. * * * * * If the people of Georgia are determined to import Slaves and make Slaves, the Federal authorities will be confined, in their efforts to suppress the traffic, wholly to the high seas, where their jurisdiction is complete." Whether this is meant as a semi-official hint from the Government to the patriotic reöpeners of the Slave Trade, that hereafter if they are only dexterous or lucky enough to evade capture at sea, and land their cargoes, its officers will not molest them, we leave for those to say who better understand the relations of the Government to the *Union*.

There is reason to apprehend that the Wanderer's cargo is not the only one of the kind, brought into the South within the year. Rumors of such importations, at different times and places, have been current; not always without an air of strong probability. Early in March, the bark E. A. Rawlins, said to belong to the owner of the Wanderer, was seized in the Bay of St. Joseph, an unfrequented place on the coast of Florida, under circumstances which left scarce a doubt that she had either just discharged a cargo of Slaves, or was preparing to sail for one. A Florida paper says, "she was higher up in St. Joseph Bay than any square-rigged vessel ever was before, and if she had Slaves aboard, had had time and opportunity to run them clear of all prying persons." Another vessel was reported, a little later, to be landing Slaves near Mobile. A letter from Jacksonville, (Fla.) about the middle of February, states that a bark left that place for Africa a few weeks before, to take in a cargo of Slaves for Florida and Georgia.

Of American vessels engaged in the traffic between Africa and Cuba, the number is indefinitely large. One of these, the Haidee, of New York, after landing her cargo of about 900 Slaves, at Cardenas, sailed northward in charge of the first

7

mate, who scuttled and sunk her off Block Island, about the middle of September; he and his crew going ashore in the boats, some to Long Island and some to Connecticut. The mate and part of the crew were shortly after arrested by the United States Marshal for New York, and lodged in jail to await examination. On the 21st of August, the brig Echo, of New Orleans, with 314 Slaves on board, was captured by the United States brig Dolphin, on the northern coast of Cuba, and sent into Charleston, where her arrival on the evening of the 27th created intense excitement. Such an event was never known before. In all the fifty years since the Foreign Slave Trade was prohibited by the nation's law, in the nearly forty years since it was branded as piracy, notorious as it has long been that American vessels were largely engaged in it, and zealous as the Government has claimed to be for its suppression, this, we believe, is the only case in which a Slaver with Slaves on board, has been taken by an American cruiser, or sent as a prize into an American port. Not Charleston only, but, as the news spread, the whole South, seemed full of the new theme. The question was at once started and warmly discussed, "what shall be done with these negroes?" True, the law had already provided *its* answer to the question, by requiring that all Slaves thus captured should be sent out of the country; but this was by no means conclusive with the questioners. "Why should we send them back?" asked a correspondent of the Charleston *Courier*, the morning after their arrival. "They are wanted everywhere; our planters, our mechanics, our railroads want them; our waste lands are in want of them. There is no reason why we should send them back, but that it is agreeable to another section of the Union to look with disgust on our institutions. * * * * * When these negroes shall be taken from the port of Charleston, (except it be to take them elsewhere in a Slave State,) it will be a brand upon our institutions that should fire the heart of every man who loves his country." A writer in the Charleston *Mercury* "shudders at the thought of their re-shipment to Africa, with all the attendant horrors of the middle passage, to say nothing of the enormous expense necessary to carry out so horrible a scheme." The Richmond *Enquirer*, also, argues stoutly for keeping and enslaving them. "To return them to Africa," it says, "is of very doubtful humanity to the negroes. To liberate them in South Carolina, and make free negro barbarians, is certainly out of the question. But one other solution remains, and that is to select masters for them, and make useful laborers of the now ignorant barbarians. What better could be done for them, *now that they are here?* We would not for one moment countenance the opening of the African Slave Trade. But an experiment may be made out of the 'Echo' cargo, that will be of great service in solving the practical usefulness of African missions. * * * * * Let upright and high-minded men be selected for their masters, and by their reports let missions to Africa be fully tested."

So eager were the good people of Charleston to realize this brilliant and benevolent idea of turning the poor " barbarians " into chattels and working tools, in order to civilize and Christianize them, and at the same time supply so many and diverse " wants " of the South, that they could not even wait for Sunday to go by, before commencing the praiseworthy task. The vessel had come in on Friday evening. Saturday, of course, could only give the kind souls time to gather up their wits, and think what should be done. So by Sunday morning they were ready to act; the urgency of the case, and the merit of the deed, no doubt dispelling any scruples about Sabbath-breaking which might disturb the consciences of so godly a community. Accordingly, that morning, several philanthropic patriots called upon the Sheriff of the District of Charleston, and with due legal formality set forth that a large number of free persons of color had been brought within his bailiwick, contrary to the South Carolina Statutes. Thereupon, the Sheriff sought legal advice, both of his own solicitor, and of the acting Attorney General of the State. The former told him he was bound to take the negroes into custody. The latter, in an elaborate written opinion, held that the case did not come within the scope of the State law, and that the negroes, being lodged in Castle Pinckney, a fort of the United States, were not within the State's jurisdiction. The Sheriff, as other men have done when their counsellors differed, acted on the advice which suited his own feelings, and forthwith sent to the United States Marshal a copy of his solicitor's opinion, and a demand for the negroes. The Marshal turned over both to the United States District Attorney, who answered the former with a copy of the acting

Attorney General's opinion, and the latter with a refusal. Castle Pinckney being too near the Charleston wharves for entire security if the Sheriff should attempt to enforce his demand, the negroes were removed to Fort Sumpter, several miles down the harbor, where they remained till arrangements were completed for sending them to Liberia, by the Steamship Niagara. About the middle of September the President concluded a contract with the American Colonization Society, by which the latter agreed to support and instruct them one year for $150 each. On the 21st they left Fort Sumpter, and were landed at Monrovia on the 30th of October, whence they have since been distributed along the coast, and placed under teachers for moral and intellectual training. Of the 455 with whom the Echo left the African coast early in July, but a little more than 200 returned to it in October. On the way to Cuba 141 died, and about 100 on the American coast, at Charleston, and on the return voyage.

The crew of the Slaver were sent to Charleston and imprisoned there, to await examination. The Captain — Townsend — was taken on board the Dolphin to Boston, and examined there, but was sent to Key West for trial, on the ground that the Dolphin had touched there, on her way northward, and that crimes committed on the high seas must be tried in the District into which the offender is first brought. We do not learn that he has yet been tried. The crew were examined on the 15th of September, and committed for trial at Columbia, in November. When the time for trial came, the Grand Jury refused to indict them, and their counsel labored earnestly to have them discharged; but the Court remanded them to jail to await the action of another Grand Jury, at the April Term, to be held in Charleston. On the 7th of April a true bill was found against them, but the trial ended in their prompt acquittal. Their counsel argued that the jury had a right to judge of the law, and that the act under which they were indicted is unconstitutional; that the term "piracy," as used in the Constitution, applies only to robbery on the high seas, and so gives Congress no power to declare Slave Trading to be piracy. Probably on this ground the Jury acquitted.

The capture of the Echo, and the judicial proceedings to which it led, brought the subject of the Slave Trade before the

South Carolina Senate, which was in session while the crew were awaiting trial. Senator MAZYCK introduced resolutions to the effect that the Federal Constitution gives Congress no power to regulate commerce among Foreign nations, "therefore all acts purporting to prohibit the Slave Trade between Foreign countries, are unconstitutional and have no force;" and that "the act of Congress declaring the Slave Trade to be piracy, as it purports to convert into piracy what is not so in the nature of things, and in the sense of the Constitution, is unconstitutional, null, and void." In a speech supporting the resolutions, he said — and truly, we think — "if Congress had the power to make the Slave Trade between Africa and Cuba piracy, it would have the same power to make the same trade piracy when carried on between Louisiana and Virginia, by way of the sea." He went farther, and showed the Slaveholder's confusion of broad moral distinctions, by contending that "the exercise of this power implies the right to declare the trade in cotton over the high seas an act of piracy," or to convert any act done on the high seas, into that crime. For "we have a right" he said, "to consider the Slave Trade as innocent and legitimate as any other trade." The resolutions were referred to the Committee on Federal Relations. What action, if any, has since been taken upon them, we have not seen.

On the 10th of November, the brig Brothers, of Charleston, S. C., was brought into that port by the sloop of war Marion, having been seized on the African coast, as a suspected Slaver; whereat the Charleston *Mercury* was highly indignant, declaring "the seizure of a vessel on suspicion " to be " a new feature introduced into our criminal code, to suppress the African Slave Trade;" and asking emphatically, "is there any Slavery equal to this, in the whole range of criminal jurisprudence? Such an atrocious novelty in law," it continues, "may win the approbation of Boston fanatics, but no jury in South Carolina, we are satisfied, will ever enforce it." The Philadelphia *Southern Monitor*, of September 11th, alludes to " the James Buchanan, a Slaver fitted out in the Delaware River, in sight of our dwelling," and adds, it "has made four successful voyages since 1856, and cleared $400,000." A correspondent of the Boston *Journal*, last summer, speaks of " having been for some time up the Congo River," which, " you are aware, is the principal rendezvous for Slaves;" so that he had "a very good opportunity of seeing into the mysteries of the Slave Trade." He says "it is a well-known fact that most of the Slave ships which visit the river are sent from New York and New Orleans." Testimony like this is abundant. And though now and then, as we have seen, a Slaver is taken by an American cruiser, yet these appear to be the rare exceptions to a very general rule. Indeed, it would almost seem that the *aim* of the Federal Government and its agents is to defeat the intent, while complying with the letter, of the treaty requiring a squadron to be kept on the coast of Africa, to suppress the Slave Trade. For, instead of several light vessels of two or three guns each — which would suit the service — a frigate is sent, carrying two-thirds or more of all the guns required, and drawing too much water to follow the Slavers into their hiding-places. And a letter from on board this frigate, published last winter, in the New York *Herald*, shows that out of fifteen months, which it had nominally passed on the coast, at the letter's date, only twenty-two days were spent on the usual cruising ground for Slavers, and thirteen of these days at anchor. Eleven months of the fifteen were whiled away at Madeira and the Cape Verds, more than three hundred miles from the coast, and nearly three thousand from that part of it which the Slavers most frequent.

The earnest purpose of Great Britain to break up the hateful traffic, the great extent to which the American flag is used in covering it, and the shameful slackness of the American Government in its duty of preventing such a disgrace to its flag, produced a state of things last spring, which, for a time, appeared almost to threaten war. A little more than a year ago, "in compliance with the wish of the American Government," (as Lord PALMERSTON has since stated in Parliament,) a British squadron was stationed on the coast of Cuba, to watch and intercept the Slave ships as they came in. Knowing how generally these ships displayed the stars and stripes as a protection; believing it was often done by vessels not American; and seeing that the artifice, if allowed success, would baffle all their efforts; the British cruisers claimed, and sometimes exercised the right of visiting suspected vessels, to ascertain their character; whether they were really American, or were false pirates, practising a fraud alike upon the country whose flag they abused, and upon that whose justice they sought to evade. From the latter part of April to the middle or latter part of May, nearly forty vessels, it is said, were visited. Of course, a howl of indignation at these "British Outrages" was raised by Cuban Slave Traders, and echoed by American Slaveholders and political demagogues; gross exaggerations and perversions of the facts were circulated; the British officers were charged with insolence and rudeness, and even brutal violence, and in one instance, at least, with having fired into an American vessel and killed a man; and no pains were spared to excite a hostile feeling toward Great Britain. That she *intended* insult and aggression was in effect assumed by the tenor of the comments on the acts complained of. Grave Senators forgot their dignity, and talked like blustering bullies. The President made haste to send to the Cuban coast every armed ship available for the purpose, with orders to resist all attempts of British cruisers to search, visit, or detain American vessels. He also demanded explanations both of Great Britain and Spain.

On the 14th of May, the Senate unanimously adopted a resolution, asking the President for information concerning the acts of the British cruisers, and what measures, if any, had been taken in relation thereto. On the 19th, the President sent documents in reply. On the 18th, the Senate unanimously adopted a resolution offered by Mr. SEWARD, instructing the Committee on Foreign Relations to inquire whether any legislation is necessary to enable the President to protect American vessels against British aggression. Mr. MASON, from that Committee, reported on the 28th, that no less than twenty-one cases of aggression had been officially made known, and accounts of fresh instances were continually arriving; argued briefly against the right of visitation, appealing to both American and English authorities; said "the Committee refrain from recommending farther legislation, only because the President has ordered all our available navy to the infested waters to protect our flag;" and closed, by announcing that the Committee had unanimously resolved, that American ships at sea, under the American flag, remain under the jurisdiction of this country, and any visitation of them is an infraction of the sovereignty of the United States; that these aggressions demand such an explanation from Great Britain as shall prevent their recurrence; and that the Committee approve

the action of the Executive, and is prepared to recommend such
future legislation as circumstances may require. The resolutions were considered on the 29th and 31st, and Senators relieved their minds of much "perilous stuff" which might else
have done them serious harm. "Honorable gentlemen" evidently thought the Committee quite too tame for the occasion.
Mr. Toombs declared their resolutions "not worth the paper they
were written on." He was in favor of an amendment offered by
Mr. HALE, to the effect that "the acts of the British are belligerent,
and should be resisted by all the power of the country;" and
further held that "the British war-ships in the Gulf should be
seized or sunk, and nothing short of this should satisfy us."
Mr. HALE thought "the acts of the British should be met by
acts and not by arguments." Mr. MALLORY liked Mr. HALE'S
amendment so well that he withdrew, in its favor, one which he
had offered. Mr. DOUGLAS asked what good it does to resolve
that these acts are belligerent. He recommended to let a ship
of war bring one of the small British cruisers into an American
port, and then it would be time for explanations. He was for
giving the President power not only to repel but to punish outrages upon our nationality. Mr. WILSON hoped that orders
had been given to sink or capture the offending ships, but also
thought we ought to see that our flag be not prostituted by
Slave Traders. Mr. HAMMOND hoped that, with or without
orders, our force in the Gulf would sink or capture one of the
offending vessels. On the 3d of June, Mr. DOUGLAS introduced
a bill to authorize the President, at his discretion, to employ the
army, and navy, and fifty thousand volunteers, and ten millions
of dollars, to resist the claims of Great Britain. But the war
fever was now abating, and after so much bellicose talk, nothing
was done looking to war. On the last day of the session the
resolutions were adopted unanimously, without amendment.
While the fever was at its height in the Senate, the other
House had a less severe attack of it, but there, too, it soon sub-
sided. A fiery speech from BURLINGAME, on the 12th of June,
called out but tame, pacific responses; and the strongest demonstration made was referring to the Committee on Foreign Affairs,
a resolution requiring the President to instruct the navy to arrest offending vessels, and hold them till reparation should be

made by the British Government. We do not learn that it was further acted on.

There were not wanting those among the onlookers, so destitute of reverent faith in Southern chivalry as to hint that the sudden subsidence of warlike ardor among the retainers of the Slave Power, was largely, if not mainly, due to the readiness with which such men as SEWARD, WILSON, HALE, and BURLINGAME seconded their patriotic zeal, instead of holding them back, as chivalry had expected; that, in short, they began to fear that blows might come of bluster, — blows from a heavier hand than Slavery likes to feel. "No forty Quakers alive," says the New York *Tribune*, "could have done so much for peace in a year, as the Senators above named did by their warlike talk during a single afternoon."

How many grains of truth were in the mass of falsehood and exaggeration which rumor brought from the Cuban coast, we cannot accurately say; but the following testimonies may throw some light upon the question. A Key West correspondent of the Charleston *Courier* quotes "Lieut. PYM," of the British gunboat Jasper, as saying "the reports of outrages on American vessels are much exaggerated, and in many instances false." Alluding to the case of the Cortes, [which was particularly referred to, by Secretary CASS, in his complaint to the British Government,] he says "the captain of that vessel, when overhauled, threw his flag into the sea and declared himself a Spaniard. The contraband articles on board proved her a Slaver, and she was accordingly sóld as such." And the New York *Tribune* says "she was known to be such before she sailed." The Boston *Traveller*, of May 28th, states that "Capt. CLINE, the boarding officer of the Merchants' Exchange Newsroom, has conversed freely with the officers and crew of every vessel from Cuba which has arrived at this port, and declares that not one of them considered himself damaged to the amount of one cent. * * * * * The British officers generally, the crews of our Cuban trade report, appeared anxious to avoid giving offence." The same paper states that "Capt. GORDON," just arrived from Sagua Grande, [the Cuban port at which most of the "outrages" are said to have been committed,] "says his brig was not troubled by the British, and he believes two-thirds of the stories about outrages, &c., are made out of whole cloth." The Boston

8

Journal, of May 24th, mentions the arrival, on that day, of two of the vessels "recently visited by British officers at Sagua." The captain of one, Capt. LAMPHER, reported that the officer who visited him asked several questions about the vessel, which were answered; and wished to see her papers, which were not shown to him, as they were on shore; he staid "about five minutes, and behaved in a very gentlemanly manner, treating the captain with all proper courtesy and respect." Capt. LAMPHER "was not offended by anything connected with the affair, and he believes that to have been the general feeling among the American shipmasters who were visited. The indignation was chiefly confined to the shore, among the Spanish officials." Capt. BRAY, of the other vessel, bears substantially the same testimony, as to the deportment of the officers who boarded him, and as to his own feeling in regard to the matter. The captain of the brig New Era, on arriving in New York, as we learn from the *Tribune*, reported that he had been boarded by one British war steamer, and fired at by another. The mates said they knew nothing of any such transaction; that one evening an officer from a British steamer hailed the captain, without boarding, politely asked the vessel's name and destination, was civilly answered, and returned to his vessel. The same paper states that the captain of the brig Mianus reported having been boarded by the British war steamer Styx, which fired a gun for him to heave to, and detained him over an hour. The mate told the reporter that no gun was fired; that an officer came on board and politely asked the customary questions, was invited to the cabin, was answered, and departed; the whole detention being about ten minutes. We gather from the Washington correspondence of the New York *Tribune*, that the President had tried, but in vain, to trace to its source the rumor about the firing into an American vessel and killing a man; that it came not from the coast, but from the interior of Georgia, and was not believed in Washington. No proof to sustain it has yet appeared. In a debate in Parliament, on the 17th of June, relating to the complaints of the American Government, the British Foreign Secretary said, "after careful examination I have not found a single instance in which our cruisers have behaved with incivility to the officers of any American vessel which they have boarded." Had there been any, we can hardly doubt the American Government would have known it, and made it known to him.

On the 9th of June came despatches from the commander of the British West India squadron, expressly disavowing having authorized the recent acts of visitation, and disclaiming having any instructions contemplating such a contingency; also stating that he had despatched a sloop to bring the offending cruisers, "intending to hold the officers to a strict account." On the 19th, despatches were received from England, announcing that the British Government, after consulting the law officers of the Crown, disclaimed, in accordance with their opinion, all right to search or visit American vessels in time of peace. But the purpose was avowed to continue the use of effective means for suppressing the Slave Trade, and the American Government was invited to suggest some plan for verifying the nationality of vessels without danger of a breach of international law. Later arrivals brought reports of long and interesting debates in Parliament, on the questions raised by the American complaint; also comments of the British Press upon the whole affair; from both of which it appears that, in disclaiming the right to search or visit vessels of a friendly nation, neither the people nor the Government intended to relinquish the right to ascertain, in cases open to strong suspicion, whether a vessel is entitled to the flag it bears; and that, in fact, *no* claim, asserted hitherto, is now surrendered. Nay more; it comes out in the debates, that from 1844 till now the British cruisers have been acting under instructions which had been approved by DANIEL WEBSTER, then Secretary of State; and were based on principles admitted by Secretary Cass, in his very letter of complaint. "The position taken by the British Government," said Mr. FITZGERALD — one of its members — "was exactly that laid down by General Cass in his letter to Lord NAPIER. In it is this passage. 'Undoubtedly, if a vessel assume a national character to which she is not entitled, she cannot be protected by this assumption. As the identity of a person must be determined at the risk of the officer bearing a process for his arrest, so must the national identity of a vessel be determined at the like hazard to him who, doubting the flag she displays, searches her to ascertain her true character. * * * * * If the boarding officer had just grounds of suspicion, and deported himself with propriety in the performance of his task, doing no injury, and peaceably retiring when satisfied of his error, no nation would make such an act the subject of serious reclamation.'" Lord JOHN RUSSELL "was happy to hear that it was not the intention of her Majesty's Government to deviate from that line of policy which we had followed for so many years." Lord PALMERSTON "concurred with Lord JOHN RUSSELL, that it was impossible to admit the naked principle that hoisting a particular flag was to be taken as unequivocal proof that the vessel belonged to the country whose flag she hoisted." If it were, "piracy of every description would roam the seas with impunity. He had not understood that the Government had adopted the principle to that extent." The Chancellor of the Exchequer, (Disraeli,) said "the Government had in no way conceded that point," but "had invited the Government of the United States to suggest the mode by which the terrible abuse of their flag might be prevented." Lord LYNDHURST said, "If one of our cruisers see a vessel with the American flag, and has reason to believe it is assumed, he must inquire into the facts as well as he can. If he ascertains, to the best of his judgment, that she has no right to the flag, he may visit and examine her papers, and, if he find his suspicion correct, may deal with her in a manner justified by the relation between England and the country to which she belongs. America would have no right to interfere. But if it should turn out that the vessel was American, we should apologize and make ample reparation for the injury committed." Lord MALMESBURY "had heard with great pleasure the views of his noble friend, because they *conform precisely to the opinion* of the law officers of the Crown, *upon which the Government had acted.*" The London *Saturday Review*, of July 31st, says, "the right of verifying the nationality of a vessel has been explicitly insisted on by every speaker who has debated the question in Parliament, and is categorically admitted by the American Minister for Foreign Affairs." On the 12th of July, a resolution was offered in the House of Commons, declaring it expedient to discontinue the practice of authorizing men-of-war to visit and search vessels under foreign flags, with a view to suppress the Slave Trade. On a division, it was lost by 24 ayes to 223 nays. In the debate upon it, Mr. FITZGERALD alluded to the admission by Mr.

Cass, of the right to ascertain the character of suspicious vessels; and said it was a right which the American Government had not scrupled to exercise; as documents which it had laid on the table of the House of Representatives showed *not less than three cases* on the coast of Africa, *in which American cruisers had searched vessels bearing the French flag.* He added, that Lord Napier, in a despatch just received, had said that Gen. Cass had told him that, "after the satisfactory declarations of the British Government, the American Government would give earnest consideration to any proposals for the verification of the nationality of vessels." In the House of Lords, on the 14th of last February, Lord Malmesbury referred to the correspondence with the United States, on the right of search. "He thought England had exercised a wise discretion in giving up that right; and he believed that a code of instructions, which had been agreed to by England and France, and had been submitted to America for approval, would be found to work satisfactorily in repressing the Slave Trade."

We may safely venture the assertion that if this "code of instructions" is really well adapted to "repressing the Slave Trade," it will *not* be approved by the American Government; or, if approved in form, for the sake of appearances, will not be carried out in action. It is not in the nature of things that Slaveholders and Slavetraders at home — and by such is this Government controlled — will be in earnest to prevent Slavetrading abroad. When the shameful and notorious prostitution of its flag to the protection of the Slave Trade shall awaken half the indignation which was "got up" at the attempt of British cruisers to prevent its fraudulent appropriation by foreign pirates to such vile uses, it will be time to hope for some hearty effort in accordance with the treaty stipulation which for five and forty years has bound the nation "to *use its best endeavors* to promote the entire abolition of the traffic in Slaves."

DOMESTIC SLAVE TRADE.

This treaty stipulation, in its terms, if not in its intent, includes the home trade, with the foreign. We do not say it was so meant; doubtless it was not understood so on this side the

water, and perhaps not on the other; but the reason given for
it by the contracting parties, that "the traffic in Slaves is
irreconcilable with humanity and justice," applies undeniably
to both alike. If, then, it is a good one for *agreeing* to abolish
one, it is *as* good for *abolishing* the other. Slaveholders themselves, as we have seen, sometimes acknowledge this; or rather
they emphatically *affirm* it, when arguing for a policy *consistently* inhuman and unjust. Why should they not be taken at
their word, when their word is so evidently true? There is no
moral difference between the foreign and the domestic trade in
Slaves, to justify us in treating this as lawful and respectable,
while rating that among the highest crimes. Nor is the
extent of the home traffic so inconsiderable; nor is the misery
it causes, in sundering friends and kindred, and scattering families, so trifling in amount or in degree, as to render it of little
moment, (if that could ever be,) whether right principles are
carried into corresponding practice in relation to it. Nor is it
kept so carefully from sight, that ignorance may excuse neglect
of duty. It is no business of byways and unfrequented cor-
ners; skulking from day, like less atrocious forms of wickedness.
It sets up its marts and warehouses on the crowded streets of
cities; flaunts its red auction-flag in the nation's face; drives its
chained coffles along the main highways; or loads its vessels at
the public wharves, and clears them regularly at the custom
houses; and freely uses the press to blazon the abundance,
quality, and cheapness of its human merchandise, and invite
dealers to its barracoons. It claims safe transit over any land
or any water which the Federal Constitution covers, be local
law or local feeling what it may; and owns no right in any
State to bar its passage or meddle with its wares. The national
Capital is still disgraced by its actual presence, though nomi-
nally it has been forbidden there; and the jails and the
newspapers of the Federal District still serve as its conven-
iences. Such notices as this which follows, copied from the
Evening Star, of Washington, are still esteemed a part of the
legitimate advertising business there; and can find place in
papers claiming to be decent, and regarded as respectable.

"ADMINISTRATOR'S SALE. — I will, in pursuance of an order
of the Orphan's Court for the District of Columbia, sell at

public auction, on Friday next, Nov. 19, at 12 o'clock, M., in front of the jail, to the highest bidder, for cash, viz:

" One negro woman and three children; one negro woman, and three likely boys from 14 to 19 years of age.

"ABSALOM A. HALL,

"Administrator of Jacob Hall."

And incidents like this, related below, can still occur within the bounds of Congressional jurisdiction.

"A striking spectacle was afforded to the street public of Washington, near the Baltimore railroad depot, on Friday. A string of Slaves, with a white man at their head, loaded pistol in hand, and another in the rear, armed in like manner, marched from some private Slavepen to the depot, to take the cars for Baltimore, where they will be sold."

How large the traffic is, now going on between the Slave-producing and the Slave-consuming States, we have no means of accurately knowing. It can hardly now be less, but probably is much greater, in amount, than in the period — from 1840 to 1850 — for which an estimate was made in 1857, by a Special Committee of the South Carolina House of Representatives. That estimate may be presumed no *over*statement; its purpose being to show the need of reöpening the Foreign Slave Trade, because the domestic could not meet the demand.   Assuming 30 per cent. as the natural increase of Slaves in those ten years, the difference between the number so obtained and the *actual* increase of Slave population in five " Slave breeding States," was found to be 235,000; which number, it was thence inferred, had been exported to the other States — an average, it will be seen, of 23,500 a year.   Reckoning their average price at $500 each, the yearly value of the trade would be ($11,750,000) nearly twelve millions of dollars.   Or rating them at the actual average price brought by PIERCE BUTLER's Slaves, over four hundred men, women, and children, sold at auction on the second and third of March last, the total value would be nearly seventeen millions of dollars [$16,644,463].   Virginia alone is estimated to have sold 111,259 Slaves, and Maryland 26,279; an average from the two States, of nearly fourteen thousand a year.   Supposing — as seems reasonable — a growth of the trade in proportion to that of the Slave population since 1850, its victims the past year must number little less than 30,000, and their total price come near to $20,000,000. This estimate, we think, more likely to be under than beyond the truth.

Perhaps no other one event, for many years, has done so much to turn attention to this traffic, or has shown to so wide a circle of beholders how detestable it is, even in its least hateful aspect, as the great auction sale of BUTLER's Slaves, to which we have just alluded. That so many Slaves, and of so generally good a quality, were exposed for sale at once; that none of them had ever been sold before, but all were born and had always lived on the estate, which was now to be so sadly broken up; that they belonged to a man residing at the North, (although of Southern birth,) and somewhat widely known; these circumstances all tended to give greater notoriety and interest to the event. The New York *Tribune* had a reporter present, whose graphic and intensely interesting picture of the scene has given to millions, it may be, a view of Slavery and its inevitable incidents, more vivid and impressive than many of them ever had before. But they who have been longest and most closely studious of its character know well that this delineation is so far from being an exaggerated picture of the traffic, as it generally appears, that it rather shows its harsher features softened down, and those which are comparatively comely set in more than usual relief. For instance, it was one condition of the sale that, instead of being offered "singly, or in lots to suit purchasers," as the common custom is, husbands and their wives, parents and their young children should be struck off together; an arrangement in which, the reporter remarks, "there is perhaps as much policy as humanity, for thereby many aged and unserviceable people are disposed of, who would not otherwise find a ready sale." Still, this, of course, did not prevent the separation of near kindred. "The man and his wife," as the reporter truly says, "might be sold to the pine woods of North Carolina, their brothers and sisters be scattered through the cotton fields of Alabama and the rice swamps of Louisiana, while the parents might be left on the old plantation to wear out their weary lives in heavy grief, and lay their heads in far-off graves, over which their children might never weep. And no account could be taken of loves that were as yet unconsummated by marriage; and how many aching hearts have been divorced by this summary proceeding, no man can ever know. And the separation is as utter, and is infinitely more hopeless, than that made by the Angel of Death, for then the loved ones are committed to the care of a merciful Deity; but in the other instance to the tender mercies of a Slavedriver."

The sale took place on the second and third of March, at the Race Course, near Savannah, Ga., where the Slaves were gathered five or six days before, that buyers might have time to examine them. "They were quartered in the sheds erected to accommodate the horses and carriages of persons who attend the races. They were huddled in, pell-mell, with no more attention to their comfort than was necessary to prevent their becoming ill and unsaleable. They ate and slept on the bare floor, there being no sign of bench or table. * * * * On the faces of all was an expression of heavy grief; * * * * few wept, the place was too public, and the drivers were too near, though some occasionally turned aside to give way to a few quiet tears. * * * * * The children were of all sizes, the youngest being fifteen days old. * * * * * For these preliminary days their shed was constantly visited by speculators. The negroes were examined with as little consideration as if they had been brutes indeed; the buyers pulling their mouths open to see their teeth, pinching their limbs to find how muscular they were, walking them up and down to detect any signs of lameness, making them stoop and bend in different ways that they might be certain there was no concealed rupture or wound; and asking them questions relative to their accomplishments."

"It seems as if every shade of character capable of being implicated in the sale of human flesh and blood was represented among the buyers. They were generally of a rough breed, siangy, profane, and bearish, being for the most part from the back river and swamp plantations. * * * * * Those who have read 'Uncle Tom,' will remember Legree. That the character is not overdrawn, there is abundant testimony. * * * * One huge brute of a man," after listening to a conversation on the management of refractory Slaves, "broke silence by saying, 'You may say what you like about managing niggers; I'm a driver myself, and I've had some experience, and I ought to know. You can manage ordinary niggers by lickin' 'em, and

9

givin' 'em a taste of the hot iron once in awhile when they 're
extra ugly, but if a nigger really sets himself up against me, I
can't never have any patience with him. I just get my pistol and
shoot him right down; and that's the best way.' And this brute
was talking to gentlemen, and his remarks were listened to with
attention, and his assertions assented to by more than one in
the knot of listeners." "But all this time the sale was going
on, and the merry auctioneer, with many a quip and jest, was
beguiling the time when the bidding was slow. The expression
on the faces of all who stepped on the block was always the
same, and told of more anguish than it is in the power of words
to express. Blighted homes, crushed hopes, and broken hearts
was the sad story to be read in all the anxious faces."

Among the "chattels" was "Daphney," with her child of
fifteen days. As the day was cold and rainy, and the place of
sale was open to the air on one side, she had been suffered to
wear "a large shawl, which she kept carefully wrapped around
her infant and herself. This *unusual* proceeding attracted much
attention, and provoked many remarks, such as these: 'What
do you keep your nigger covered up for? pull off her blanket;'
'What's the fault of the gal? ain't she sound? Pull off her
rags, and let us see her;' and a loud chorus of similar remarks,
emphasized with profanity, and mingled with sayings too indecent and obscene to be even hinted at here, went up from the
crowd of chivalrous Southern gentlemen." "Look at the circumstances of this case. The day was the second day of
March. Daphney's baby was born into the world on St. Valen-
tine's happy day, the 14th of February. Since her confinement
Daphney had travelled from the plantation to Savannah, where
she had been kept in a shed for six days. On the sixth or
seventh day after her sickness, she had left her bed, taken a
railroad journey across the country to the shambles, was there
exposed for six days to the questionings and insults of the negro
speculators, and then on the fifteenth day after her confinement
was put upon the block, with her husband and her other child,
and, with her new-born baby in her arms, sold to the highest
bidder."

Deeply pathetic is the story the reporter tells of "Jeffrey"
and his betrothed; of Jeffrey's earnest pleading with the master who had bought him, to buy Dorcas, too; of the half

promise which his importunity obtains; of the smiles which brighten two dark faces, and the hope and joy which lighten two loving hearts; then of the "long hours of feverish suspense," till, on the second day of sale, Dorcas is brought out; and lastly, of the crushing of their hopes by the discovery that Dorcas is not to be sold alone, and Jeffrey's master will not buy the family to which she belongs. "Jeffrey reads his doom in his master's look, and turns away, the tears streaming down his honest face. So Dorcas is sold, and her toiling life is to be spent in the cotton fields of South Carolina, while Jeffrey goes to the rice plantation of the Great Swamp. To-morrow they are to say their tearful farewell, and go their separate ways, to meet no more as mortal beings. But didn't Mr. BUTLER give them a silver dollar apiece? Who shall say there is no magnanimity in Slaveowners?"

"And so the Great Sale went on for two long days, during which time were sold four hundred and twenty-nine men, women, and children. There were some thirty babies in the lot; esteemed worth to their master a hundred dollars the day they are born, and to increase in value at the rate of a hundred dollars a year till they are sixteen or seventeen years old. The total amount of the sale foots up $303,850." The prices ranged from $1750 for "a fair carpenter and caulker," down to $250 each for a gray-haired couple, old and sick. The average, it will be seen, was a little over $700 each. After the sale was over, Mr. BUTLER "of the free city of Philadelphia, was solacing the wounded hearts of the people he had sold from their homes," by giving to each "a dollar in specie;" having "bags of twenty-five cent pieces, fresh from the mint, to give an additional glitter to his generosity."

"And now come the scenes of the last partings — of the final separations of those who were akin, or who had been such dear friends from youth that no ties of kindred could bind them closer — of those who were all in all to each other, and for whose bleeding hearts there shall be no earthly comfort — the parting of parents and children, of brother from brother, and the rending of sister from a sister's bosom; and O, hardest, cruelest of all, the tearing asunder of loving hearts, wedded in all save the one ceremony of the Church — these scenes pass all description; it is not meet for pen to meddle with tears so holy."

The spirited sketch from which we have been extracting, went across the water, and was extensively republished by the British press. The London *Times*, referring to it, said, "it is a long time since we have seen anything which photographed the Slave-dealing system so completely as the description which we printed yesterday, of a large sale of Slaves, at Savannah, Georgia. The whole melancholy drama of Slave life is displayed before the reader; from the ruin of the speculative Southern gentleman whose hereditary estate must be sold for the benefit of New York creditors, to the dispersion of the Slaves among other masters, some petty, grasping tyrants, very different from the old caste of which the South still continues to be proud, though with less reason than formerly. * * * * * If any one wishes to see how low the white man can be brought by unlimited power to use human beings for gain, let him read the life-like description of the Southern planters, and see into what a class the increase of the cotton trade has changed the gentlemen of the Carolinas and Georgia."

A notice of the domestic Slave Trade would be incomplete, without at least a brief allusion to one feature of it, worse than any brought to view in the preceding pages; and setting in a stronger light the terribly depraving and dehumanizing influence of Slavery. It is horrible that the pirate of the Guinea coast tears from a parent's arms the shrieking child, and sunders brothers and sisters from each other, to gratify his lust of gain; horrible that "the merry auctioneer" of the domestic trade, "with many a quip and jest" brings down on throbbing hearts the hammer stroke which rudely severs those whom natural affection and the nearest consanguinity have closely bound together; but what words can speak the abhorrence due to the notorious fact, that, in this "free, enlightened, Christian land," men sell their own children and their father's children to the toil unpaid, the suffering unpitied, and the debasement ineffable and inevitable, which appertain to chattel Slavery? The Slave Code cunningly adopts the principle that the child shall follow the condition of the mother; and so, by making the Slave mother's child her master's property, allies against her, in the master's breast, two passions which are wont elsewhere to counteract and check each other; and enhances fearfully the tendency of the Slave system to demoralize the master and debase the Slave. Moreover — what at once reveals and aggravates the evil — the more the vice is practiced, to which the marketable quality of its product tempts, the stronger the temptation grows; for an infusion of the paler blood augments the money value of a female Slave, — the white man's chattel daughter brings a higher price than the black man's daughter. Thus the domestic trade not only is the same in essence as the foreign, involving the same disregard of human rights and feelings; as truly, in its *moral* elements, piratical; it also has its own peculiar wickedness, its special means and methods of corruption; opening, as it does, a way to make money out of vice, by turning its results into articles of traffic.

KIDNAPPING.

From Slave Trading, whether in the foreign or the domestic "article;" or from Slaveholding, whether of Congo negroes, freshly imported, or natives of Virginia, of half a dozen descents, and crossed or not crossed with "the best blood of Virginia," the moral distance is not great, nor the transition intrinsically difficult, to that method of procuring Slaves, which may be called a recurrence to first principles, but which "unconquered prejudice" would style kidnapping, namely, the stealing of men and women whom even Slaveholders' law confesses to be free. For, in truth, the latter have no more right to freedom than the former. If the former lost their right, beyond recovery, by being once seized and sold, why should not the like process with the latter yield the same result; or, to give the argument a slightly different turn, if the old theft of a century or two ago could impart so durable a title that it is not yet worn out, why should not the fresh theft of to-day confer at least as good a title? The legal sanction in the one case, and its absence in the other, make no essential difference; for most men *feel*, even if they do not clearly see, that law can neither make nor unmake right; although experience proves abundantly that, by authorizing wrong within a certain limit, it trains men to do wrong beyond that limit. Besides, the elder wrong was just as lawless as the later, at the outset; and shaped the law to suit itself, as it grew up to power; so from that *lawless* wrong the present

"legal right" is derived. Why, then, may not the present lawless wrong become in time a "legal right?" We have every
reason, therefore, to expect among the fruits of Slavery, frequent
attempts to kidnap freemen. Nor do the facts disappoint such
expectation. Cases occur, no doubt, of which we never hear;
more, possibly, remain unknown than come to light. Sometimes
a case is revealed years after its occurrence; its long conceal-
ment hinting at the likelihood that others, many more, perhaps,
have happened, which we never know. But we hear of quite
enough to prove that mere human nature, with its rights, is really
respected in *no* man, where it is not respected in *every* man;
and that if some men are still measurably safe in a Slaveholding
country, it is for other reasons than that, being men, they have
the common rights of manhood.

On the 7th of last June, a woman was arrested in New
Albany, Ind., for having sold a free colored girl, three years
old, to a family about removing to Missouri. She was held to
bail to await examination, but virtually confessed her guilt by
forfeiting her bond. On the 12th of August, a verdict was given
in Mason County, Ky., which restored to freedom a young
white woman, who had been illegally enslaved more than twenty years before, by her own father. When she was born he
took her from her free white mother, and placed her with one
of his Slaves, a light mulatto woman, whom he compelled by
threats to keep her parentage a secret, while rearing her as her
own. After his death, his widow sent the girl to a Slave prison,
intending to sell her to go South; but her fair complexion
caused suspicion and led to inquiries; the facts came out; and
a suit for her freedom was brought, with the result which we
have mentioned. The Shawneetown *Illinoian* relates a case
which happened in its neighborhood, wherein murder was probably added to man-stealing. A young negro man was seized
near Shawneetown, (just across the river from Kentucky,) and,
without legal process, carried to the Kentucky side, although
he claimed to be a freeman and a native of Indiana, (whence
he had but just arrived,) and told such facts and circumstances
to confirm his story, as left, the *Illinoian* says, "no doubt upon
the minds of the large mass of our citizens that he was free."
Some faint remonstrance seems to have been made against the
lawless outrage, but no resolute resistance was offered to it.

The perpetrators came back the next day and said their captive had escaped, and they had pursued him into the river and lost sight of him. He was found dead the following day, drifted by the waves to the Kentucky shore. The Wilmington, Del. *Commonwealth* states that in July or August two negro boys were entrapped by some persons, in Sussex County, in that State, and sold into Slavery in Virginia. But efforts made to trace them were happily successful, and they have doubtless been restored to their homes and freedom. The Charleston, S. C. *Courier* tells the story of a boy, fourteen or fifteen years old, claiming " to be white and free," who was offered for sale in St. Augustine, Fla., on the 4th of September, having been stolen, he said, from Charleston, " summer before last," by a steamboat engineer, who lured him on board the boat with the offer of a biscuit. ·He was taken to a negro trader in Savannah, who sold him; and he had since passed through seven or eight hands before he was brought to St. Augustine. He was taken in charge by the authorities, to await the procuring of testimony from Charleston, as to the correctness of his statements. We have not seen the issue of the case. The following case was published last October, in the *Vox Populi*, of Lowell, Mass. If truly stated, it involves a flagrant breach of trust, a gross, pecuniary fraud, with the higher crime of kidnapping. A colored woman, Betsey, and her daughter, Caroline, made a complaint before J. N. MORSE, Esq., of Lowell, averring that they had once been Slaves; that about six years ago their master, JESSE CORNWELL, a rich Mississippi planter, who was also father of the younger woman, died; that on his death-bed he requested his friend, Dr. KEYES, to take charge of his effects, including a large sum of money, and to convey the women to a Free State and see them comfortably settled there, and for that purpose to take $5,000, divide $4,000 equally between the mother and the daughter, and to retain $1,000 for his services; that after CORNWELL's death, KEYES hired them out six years at $100 a year, each; then brought them, in the latter part of May last, to Lowell, where they had since lived in his family, under strict surveillance. Upon this statement MORSE brought a suit against KEYES, for the recovery of the money given by CORN-WELL, and for the wages of their six years' labor. KEYES was arrested and held to bail in $6,000. He claimed that CORN-

WELL gave the women to him! But the case was not allowed
to come into court. Before the time of trial, KEYES made a
compromise with the counsel for the women, by which he gave
to the said women a life lease in a small house in Lowell, and
agreed to pay them a fixed sum of money semi-annually, thus
virtually confessing judgment against himself, and confirming
the essential truth of the women's statement. The women are
now free, and beyond the power of this wretch, but the audacity
of the attempt to hold them as Slaves, in Massachusetts, and its
success, for a time, should be a warning to every friend of Freedom to employ the strictest vigilance, and to suffer no doubtful
case to go unchallenged. A correspondent of the New York
Tribune, writing from Wheeling, Va., on the 29th of November,
speaks of a tavern-keeper, in that city, who, some years ago,
sold into Slavery, down the Mississippi river, a free negro boy
who had been bound to him for a term of years. "The fact
leaked out, legal proceedings were instituted," and the boy was
restored to freedom. Some weeks ago, a free negro woman,
who worked in the tavern-keeper's kitchen, mysteriously disappeared with her two children. It has since been learned that
she was decoyed, at her master's instance, on board a boat
going down the river, and, with her children, sold to Slavery in
Kentucky. On the 8th of December, a young colored man, in
New York, named SIMPSON, was accosted in the street, and
induced to ship himself as a seaman on a vessel bound, professedly, to Liverpool. After he had signed the shipping papers
and gone on board, an order for his half-pay, sent to his mother,
and by her presented at the shipping-office, was declared to be
spurious. This rousing her suspicion of some evil design upon
her boy, she applied to the Mayor, who set the police at once to
looking into the affair. The ship was boarded, and the crew
ordered on deck; when it was found composed entirely of colored boys, no white men, but the mates, being on board; the
boys had no free papers, and the voyage was to be to Mobile,
instead of Liverpool. SIMPSON was taken before the Mayor
and released. These facts we gather from the New York *Tribune*. It adds, "the Sergeant of the harbor police says he has
frequently known ships to sail for southern ports with colored
crews, and has noted it as a remarkable fact, that none of the
crews ever came back."

A case which created much local excitement has been twice tried within the year, at Pittsburg, Pa. It was that of George Shaw, accused of kidnapping a white mechanic, of that city, named Ferris; by enticing him to St. Louis, and delivering him to a man who claimed that he was in part of negro blood, and a fugitive Slave from Alabama. The crime was instigated by a reward of $500. Its commission, and the perpetrator's boast of his success, were fully proved; and it was not pretended that he had acted under any legal warrant, or had used any of the legal forms required for the recovery of runaway Slaves. It was a deed of private villany,— its atrocity enhanced not only by the cool treachery which consummated it, but by the circumstance that it bereft a wife and young child of husband and father, leaving the worse than widowed woman in the deepest distress. The defence proposed to prove that Ferris had been a Slave in Alabama. To this it was objected that it must first be proved, and by the *best* evidence the case admits of— a certified copy of the law itself— that Slaves are held in Alabama, "under the laws thereof." The Court, very properly, sustained the objection, and promptly overruled, as fast as they were tried, the various devices of the prisoner's counsel to escape the consequences of this requirement. The prisoner was convicted after a brief conference by the jury, and evidently to general satisfaction in that region. The Pittsburg *Gazette* thus comments on the case and its result.

"The law was made for crushing just such creatures as that Shaw. He is worse in society than a pestilence. Does any one imagine that if any Slaveholder in Alabama were to send him $500 to steal him a man and deliver him, that Shaw would wait to inquire whether the man he could get had ever been a Slave? The fact that Ferris had been a Slave, if it were a fact, did not in the least palliate Shaw's crime. There is a most odious law on the statute books by which he might have robbed Ferris of himself and been held blameless. Not choosing to shield himself even behind that, he has met a kidnapper's reward, and will doubtless receive at the hands of a just judge the punishment which a crime so base deserves."

This expectation was disappointed. For some informality in the proceedings, a new trial was granted. It came off last April, resulting in acquittal. Thus while his innocent victim remains

10

in hopeless Slavery, the treacherous man-stealer, the spoiler of the domestic sanctuary, escapes the penalty of human law. But, after all, his was no profitable villany, even if God's law is left out of the account. Even if conscience has no sting for him, and baseness saves him from the sense of infamy; the lawyer's fees must have dipped deeply into those $500 of blood money — for work, like that his counsel had to do, would seem to need, and probably received, large wages — and the residue would be scant payment for almost a year's imprisonment, from his arrest to his acquittal.

PERSECUTION OF THE FREE COLORED PEOPLE.

Schemes of a sort of *wholesale* kidnapping, by State authority, are recommended in some portions of the South, and have even begun to be adopted. Last winter the Legislature of Arkansas passed an act to drive out or enslave all the free negroes of that State. Those who refuse to go before the 1st of January, 1860, are graciously permitted to choose for themselves masters who shall not sell them, and for whose debts they shall not be liable to be seized, and who shall pay into the Common School Fund one-half the price at which the County Court shall have had them apprized. Bills substantially like this have been introduced into the Legislatures of North Carolina and Missouri. Arkansas has also passed an act, forbidding, after January 1st, 1860, the employment of free colored persons on the water craft navigating the rivers of that State, and subjecting the employer to a fine of from $500 to $1000, and imprisonment not exceeding twelve months. Ohio has passed an act forbidding "persons in whole or in part of African descent," to vote. The penalty is imprisonment from one to six months, and fine of not over $500. In Louisiana, the Slaveholders of the parish of St. Landry lately met and recommended that an act be passed, providing that hereafter all free colored persons, convicted of any offence against the laws, shall be sold into Slavery, for life, or for a term of years, according to the nature of the offence. The Grand Jury of Chesterfield District, South Carolina, at the recent term of the Court of Common Pleas, presented the free negroes of the District as a nuisance, and recommended " that the Legislature pass some law which will relieve the community of this troublesome population." The Cheraw *Gazette* is "pleased with this act of the Grand Jury, and hopes other Grand Juries will follow the example" till the law makers will "abate the nuisance." In Maryland, during last summer and fall, several County Conventions were held, at whose suggestion a general Convention for the Eastern Shore assembled at Cambridge, on the 3d of November, and continued in session two days, to consider what measures ought to be adopted in regard to the free colored people. Judge STEWART, of Dorchester, said, "the manumission of Slaves has been a great error, and an evil to themselves as well as to the master and the Slave. The free negroes must, therefore, gradually, and by the most reasonable steps, be brought back to their original condition. * * * * * This should be the primary duty of the next Legislature, and they should meet it manfully and without hesitation." ELIAS GRISWOLD, of Dorchester, "entirely approved of the views so ably urged by Judge STEWART," and proposed "a Committee to report resolutions for action." Col. HAMBLETON, of Talbot, thought the people of that County "would acquiesce in whatever might be here adopted to subject the free negro population to proper control. He was ready to pledge their entire coöperation." Col. JACOBS, of Worcester County, thought "that the question of restoring the free negroes to servitude, if they persisted in remaining in the State, should at once be avowed as the only remedy for the evils complained of." Resolutions were unanimously adopted, vilifying the free colored people ; declaring that "Maryland is, *and of right ought to continue*, a Slaveholding State, and that free negroism and Slavery are incompatible with each other, and should not be permitted longer to exist in their present relations within the State ; " calling for "prompt and effective legislation on the subject; " inviting a State Convention to meet at Baltimore on the second Wednesday in June, 1859, to devise some plan for the regulation of the negro population, to be presented to the Legislature ; and suggesting, as the plan to be considered, "that the State should present the alternative, to this class of our population, of going into Slavery or leaving the State." In the Board of Aldermen, of Washington, (within the range of the "exclusive legislation" of Congress, be it noted,) a bill has been introduced, requiring all

76 REPORT.

free colored persons over twelve years old to register their names and pay five dollars for permission to reside in the city a year, or in default, to be fined ten dollars and imprisoned ninety days; the penalty to be repeated as often as ten days after its infliction shall go by without compliance with the law.

ALLEGED NEGRO INCAPACITY.

As these and kindred measures of injustice are defended by alleging that the negro race is naturally incapable of using freedom rightly; is indolent and thriftless, given to animal indulgence, with a strong proclivity to vice and crime, and no aptitude for generous culture; it may not be amiss to cite some facts and testimonies, bearing on this point, which we have happened on within the year. The New Orleans *True Delta*, speaking of these measures and the disposition shown in Louisiana to adopt them, says of the free negroes there, "There is a large native resident population, correct in their general deportment, honorable in their intercourse with society, and free from reproach so far as the laws are concerned, not surpassed in the inoffensiveness of their lives by any equal number of persons in any place, North or South." The Little Rock *Gazette*, the "Democratic" organ of Arkansas, thus speaks of "Mr. HENRY KING," who is compelled, by the recent law of that "Democratic" State, to advertise his property therein for sale, because he is of the proscribed complexion. "We have known him from our boyhood, and take the greatest pleasure in testifying to his good character. The community in which he casts his lot will always be blessed with that 'noblest work of God,' 'an honest man.'" [What, then, are they who drove him from his home, and robbed themselves of that blessing?] Cincinnati papers of last June mention the purchase of a Slave to freedom by his sister, ALICE WILLIAMS, of that city, "for $950, which she has been accumulating for that purpose, ever since she became free, nine or ten years ago." How idle and worthless she must have been, all that time! WILLIAM GOODELL, writing on the 19th of November last, to the New York *Times*, quotes from the New York Metropolitan Police Report a statement that the "total number of arrests" in that city, within the year preceding, was

"60,885," and "among these were 566 colored persons." He then goes on to show that as the colored people were in 1850, by actual enumeration, about 2.68 per cent. of the whole population, and probably still hold about the same proportion, the amount of crime disclosed among them is little more than one-third as great, according to their numbers, as that among the whites. Almost exactly as .91 to 2.68, or 34 per cent.

On the second of August, a Convention of colored people celebrated, in New Bedford, Mass., the Anniversary of West India Emancipation. Many of the Massachusetts papers attest the highly respectable character of the Convention, and the high order of talent and eloquence which it exhibited. A correspondent of the New York *Tribune* says it was "a demonstration of their capacity to conduct themselves with propriety, to manage public assemblies with success, and to speak with eloquence and humor. * * * * Judging by the looks of the Convention, there are a great many colored people in the cities and towns of this State who are comfortably off in the world, enjoying many rights and privileges, though still under the ban of prejudice to a certain extent." We refer to this Convention, because we chanced to meet a notice of it while the present topic is before us; and not because it is the only one, by many, in which the colored people of the North have shown that where the Anti-Slavery movement has secured for them, in some good degree, an opportunity to improve themselves, they are rising in intelligence and moral worth, and vindicating for themselves an honest reputation. We may further say, as to the intellectual capability of the "inferior race," that while IRA ALDRIDGE is astonishing and delighting the most cultivated minds of Europe, by his triumphs on the stage; while the young Haitien students, FAUBERT, DELVA, and DUPUY, are bearing off the highest or "grand prize of honor," and the first prizes in Greek and Latin, from all their white competitors, at the concourse, in Paris, of all the colleges of France, and the first victor is deemed worthy of a military escort to a public dinner with the Minister of Public Instruction, a seat at table next a Prince of the Imperial family, and a liberal gift of handsomely bound books from the Emperor himself, (and tokens such as these, in France, mean something;) while another colored man, GIRARD, Professor in the University of Paris, is mentioned by the Paris press as "one of the very few laureates of the University who have obtained successively at the Sorbonne the two prizes of Rhetoric and Philosophy;" while colored men, in our own country, of humbler pretensions and less favored by circumstances, are displaying ingenuity and inventive power which attract the commendation of scientific journals,— as in the case of DIETZ's plan for a Broadway railroad; or which secure certificates of confidence in the utility of their inventions from municipal chief magistrates, and induce practical men to invest money in realizing their schemes, as in the case of the fire-extinguishing apparatus of AARON ROBERTS, of Philadelphia, favorably mentioned by the New York *Journal of Commerce*,— to say nothing of the multitude of other indications of the black man's capacity for mental culture and improvement which are meeting us continually wherever a fair chance to test it has been given; the confident deniers of it would do well to ask themselves, whether the proofs they think he gives of incapacity are due to his fault or their own; whether *they* are not trying to take advantage of their own wrong, to justify the continuance and aggravation of the wrong.

MANUMISSIONS.

The Slaveholders have not all adopted, yet, Judge STEWART's doctrine that manumitting Slaves is a great mistake; for instances of manumission have been scattered all along the year. Hoping that the number much exceeds our knowledge, we mention such as we have heard of. The first is that of Hannah, a Slave of DAVID JAMESON, of Memphis, Tenn., who emancipated her last June, in Cincinnati. Next, in July, two women and their five children, brought to that city from Louisiana by their masters, were set free in the Court of Common Pleas. Also in the Court of Probate, a Mr. FAULKNER, of Tennessee, emancipated a woman and her son and daughter. In the same month, a woman and her five children, to whom a Mrs. PERRY, of North Carolina, had, by her will, given freedom, and $10,000, were brought to Cleveland, and an arrangement was made with Judge TILDEN, of that city, to receive the money for them, and assist them in investing it. In August, a Missis-

sippi planter, named MOTLEY, emancipated, in the Cincinnati
Probate Court, a boy whom he acknowledged as his son; intending to give him the best education he can in this country,
and then send him to Europe. September gives us several
cases. Forty-nine Slaves from Fayette County, Ky., mostly
women and children, emancipated by their mistress, were sent
to a colony of emancipated Slaves, in Green County, Ohio. The
colony, with this addition, numbers 849. S. S. GRIFFING, of
Louisiana, emancipated, in Cincinnati, a woman and her two
children. "A hard-fisted, rough, white laborer," says the Cincinnati *Gazette*, "is in this city to record deeds of emancipation
for a woman and her [and his] five children. He came from
Arkansas, leaving there some property, because his conscience
would no longer allow him to hold his wife in Slavery. He has
exhausted his ready money," but "is bravely endeavoring to get
work, even the humblest, preferring freedom and poverty to
comfortable circumstances in the midst of Slavery." In March,
one ROBERT BARNETT, of Lincoln County, Ky., emancipated in
the Cincinnati Probate Court nine male and nine female Slaves,
a father, mother, and their children, and grandchildren, and a
woman with four boys. "In Covington, before crossing the
river, he was offered $20,000 for them, but he quietly remarked,
'I would not take fifty thousand.'" Also, in March, in the same
Court, a young woman, Agnes Wright, "whom no one would
suspect of having African blood in her veins," was manumitted
by her master, REUBEN WRIGHT, of New Orleans. About the
same time, SIDNEY WEBB, of Fairfax County, Va., removed
into Wisconsin, taking with him four Slaves, whom he emancipated and provided for. In April, eleven Slaves, from North
Carolina, passed through St. Louis, on their way to Kansas or
Nebraska, in pursuance of their lately deceased master's will,
which ordered that they should be taken into one of the Territories, and there be set free, and provided with land enough for
their support, and all necessary farming implements. A letter,
written in April, to the *Anti-Slavery Standard*, speaking of the
writer's recent visit to Virginia, says: "While I was in Fredericksburg, one of its citizens, a man, too, of honorable position,
was absent in a free State, settling five of his children and their
mother. They were all, by Virginia law, Slaves, and he was
obliged to take them out of the State."

This list of manumissions would have been much lengthened, probably much more than doubled, but for the new legal doctrines which Southern Courts are introducing to defeat the plain, well-known intentions of testators, wishing to bequeath freedom to their Slaves. A case occurred in Georgia, last summer, in which the Court decided that a will bequeathing Slaves to a legatee for his life, and directing that they should after that be freed and sent to a Free State, or Liberia, is void under the emancipation acts of Georgia, because, in legal contemplation, its effect would be the *instant* liberation of the Slaves in Georgia, on termination of their life estate; which, being contrary to the spirit and policy of the laws of Georgia on the subject, is not to be allowed. Thus, by a legal fiction, or at best a mere abstraction, the Slaves are robbed of freedom, and the master— to a south-side view — of power to do what he thinks right or best with his own lawful property.

Virginia is taking the same course, lessening the chance of Slaves to profit by testamentary gifts of freedom. Her first judicial step in that direction, if we mistake not, was taken near the close of 1857, by a decision on the will of one POIN-DEXTER, giving his Slaves "the choice of being emancipated, or sold publicly." The questions raised were, whether this was an absolute emancipation, or — if dependent on their choice — whether they had a legal right to choose. The Circuit Court deciding that it was an absolute emancipation, and their choice need not be asked; an appeal was taken to the Supreme Court of Appeals, where it was argued, held under consideration from the Spring Term to the Fall Term, reärgued, and at last decided, by three Judges against two, that the will did not emancipate the Slaves, but gave them a mere choice between Slavery and Freedom; that their act of election was a condition precedent to their becoming free; that this involved the exercise of civil and social rights, and legal capacity; and that "Slaves *have no civil or social rights,* no legal capacity to make, discharge, or assent to contracts," and therefore cannot "exercise an election in respect to manumission;" and consequently that the negroes in this case continued to be Slaves. As this decision, in the words of the Richmond *Enquirer*, "reverses the mistaken philanthropy of former decisions," — and is not supported, we believe, by a single precedent — the Judge who delivered it finding it expedient to treat "the question as one to be tested by the general principles pertaining to the subject, and not as one controlled by the influence of a special adjudication"— and as two Judges of the five dissented, one in "an able and earnest opinion, fully expressing his opposing views," the other with a simple reference to preceding cases, as having "settled the question in favor of the Slaves;" there seemed some room for doubt whether the new doctrine had yet acquired the force of law. "Under these circumstances," says the *Enquirer*, "it became a matter of great professional interest, and of public importance, to know whether the decision of the majority of the Court would be acknowledged in any future case, by the dissenting Judges, as binding authority." The earlier decisions had been regarded as establishing the point that giving Slaves, by will, the choice of Slavery or Freedom, emancipates them absolutely; and "under their supposed authority," the *Enquirer* says, "wills had been drawn all over the State." Hence "the expected freedom of thousands, to whom election had been given, depended upon the decision of this case."

At the spring term, nearly a year ago, the question was again decided, in a case which the *Enquirer* thinks "the most important to the institution of negro Slavery that has been adjudicated since the times of Lord MANSFIELD." While the Poindexter case was pending, and the law of testamentary emancipation stood on its own basis, a Mrs. COULTER died, leaving a large estate, and ninety-six Slaves, whom she had meant to free by will. To this end she had employed one of the best lawyers in the county, to express her intention in due legal form; and had submitted his work to a Judge of the Court of Appeals, who pronounced it without flaw. She directed that the Slaves be manumitted on the 1st of January, 1858, and a sufficient fund be raised from the estate to remove them to, and settle them in Liberia, or any other Free State or country in which they should choose to live; adding, "if any of them shall prefer to remain in Virginia, it is my desire that they shall be permitted to select their owners among my relatives." The Circuit Court of the County, on a bill filed by the executors

11

asking it to construe the will, decided that the Slaves were free, unless they declined to accept freedom. None of them declined; and it was generally thought that their freedom was secure. Only a few years before, the Court of Appeals had decided that certain Slaves were absolutely emancipated by a will directing their emancipation at a designated time, but providing that should they "prefer remaining in the State, they can do so by choosing masters to serve during the life of the person chosen, at whose death they shall have the option of Freedom or Slavery, by making a second choice;"—and Mrs. COULTER's will was deemed, almost beyond a doubt, the same in substance as this, and virtually sustained, of course, by the same decision. But Slavery has sharp eyes for nice distinctions, when her title to such a wealth of human bones and muscles hangs upon them. A lawyer astute enough to see "that a very clear distinction could be drawn between the two cases," advised an appeal; and legatees sufficiently unscrupulous and selfish to value gain of gold above the rights of the weak and poor, above the dying wishes of the relative who had enriched them, were prompt to act on the advice; and the same Judges who, six months before, "reversed the mistaken philanthropy" of their predecessors, again decided in the oppressor's favor. As in the former instance, three Judges against two sustained the appeal. They held the doctrine of the Poindexter case to be settled law; that Mrs. COULTER's will comes within its operation; and that her Slaves, having no legal capacity to make the choice proposed to them, are therefore still in Slavery. "It is now presumed," the *Enquirer* says, "that all the Judges will hereafter recognize that principle as controlling authority in all future cases of the kind." The Richmond *Examiner*, with which the *Enquirer* expresses its concurrence, hails the decision, with evident satisfaction, as having practically decided that "Slavery is desirable for the South, desirable for the Slave, and right in itself;" and the *Enquirer* takes it as a declaration, by the Supreme Court of Appeals, that the people of Virginia are "fully and thoroughly in favor of the institution of Slavery." It may be worth an incidental mention, that the lawyer who had drawn the will, and thus had pledged his faith and honor that it should be legally sufficient to effect the testator's intention, was counsel for the legatees in getting it annulled.

Among the Slaves thus cheated of their freedom by a process with which, we think, the deeds of common swindlers or pickpockets would honorably compare, were five, whose case has since awakened at the North effective sympathy; Ellen, the daughter of a white father, and a mother almost white, and her four children, who have also a white father. Her mother, too, was among the victims of the "legal" fraud; but was not admitted to the favored group. When asked by her new master if she would stay on the estate, — which all, it seems, who chose it, were allowed to do, although "incapable of making an election," — she so forgot the difference between a woman and a chattel, or possibly was so unmindful of the "clear distinction," which shrewd lawyers and grave judges see between a robbery with forms of law and one without such forms, as to let out her burning sense of wrong and bitter disappointment, in the indignant answer, "No, I would sooner die than remain with you another day." So she was straightway sold to Alabama. As Ellen's father was a prominent citizen of Fredericksburg, and an acquaintance of the planter whom the Virginia Court had helped to steal her and her children, the planter, in the fulness of his friendly generosity, offered to sell them, to be freed, for $1,000, only two-fifths of their estimated market value. A negro trader bought them, and permitted Ellen to go North and raise the money to redeem them. Her mission was successful, and they now are free.

The newspapers mention a suit for freedom which has been in the Missouri Courts for sixteen years. The plaintiff, Charlotte, claimed as a Slave by one CHOUTEAU, has four times gained her cause in the lower Court; and as often it has been appealed. Three times it has been sent back for a new trial; the Supreme Court — if its ruling is correctly stated — seeming to shift its ground on purpose to defeat her claim; holding the Court below to be in error, the first time in deciding that the law of Canada concerning Slavery was matter for the Court and not the Jury to consider; the second time, in deciding that it was for the Jury and not the Court; and the third time as the first. Decision on the fourth appeal is not yet announced. The defendant is said to be a millionaire, and yet he cannot afford to let one poor woman, whom he calls his property, enjoy in peace the right to herself which the Courts award her.

FUGITIVE SLAVE CASES.

It will not be thought strange that the Slaves are not always disposed to wait for either their masters or the Courts to give them freedom, but sometimes try, instead, to take it for themselves, when opportunity occurs for doing so in a quiet, unobtrusive way. The "Underground Railroad" appears to have been doing a large, and generally successful business, during the year. We hear of frequent emigrations northward, and of comparatively few returns. Indeed, the frequency of self-emancipation by this method is one avowed main reason for the movements lately made, in several Slave States, to drive out or enslave the free colored people. They are suspected of assisting in the secret exodus of their brethren from the house of bondage; and it is thought, no doubt, a profitable if not a righteous mode of punishing that crime, to put the offender in the place which he has helped another to vacate.

One thing is noticeable, unless we err, in regard to these escapes of Slaves; that oftener, lately, than in former years, numbers go off together. Last June, for instance, one Southern paper told of "nine or twelve" who had left Loudon County, Virginia, in a body; in August, comes another with the news of "ten in one stampede from Barbour County;" and a week later, four are off from Hampshire County. Then, in November, ten escaping from Virginia, were overtaken in Fayette County, Pennsylvania, when a desperate fight ensued, and the pursuers were driven back; one master owing his return alive to one of his own Slaves in the escaping party, who stepped in to protect him from another Slave's attack. The next news of the fugitives — no longer Slaves — is of their reaching Canada about the end of the month. A company of seventy from Missouri, as the Keokuk *Gazette* informs us, passed on a Sunday morning, near the end of March, through Burlington, Iowa, on their way to a land of freedom.

Some instances of narrow escape from recapture are mentioned. One, which occured last spring, in Cincinnati, was of "a perfectly white woman" from Kentucky, "so Caucasian in appearance," says the Cincinnati *Gazette*, that she traveled unsuspected on the cars from Lexington. Her master's son and two or three other men pursued, and finding her one Sunday evening in the street, returning from a religious meeting with several other women, tried to seize her. She resisted stoutly, and, while two policemen who came up were remonstrating with the men for "abusing the ladies," she slipped off without waiting for them to explain, and was next heard of at the northern terminus of the "Underground." Last fall, a man and his wife, from Missouri, were followed to Chicago, and traced to the house at which they had stopped; but they passed out at a back door while their pursuers were watching the house, and made good their retreat to Canada. In September last, a man escaped from Wilmington, North Carolina, by hiding in a vessel bound for some port in Connecticut. When found, he had been twelve days on board, living on "two pounds of crackers and a piece of cheese." Arriving shortly after, off the entrance of Mystic river, he swam ashore while the captain was gone to find an officer in whose charge to place him. The captain hastened to New London to make efforts for retaking him, and happening to find him there, brought him at once before a United States Commissioner, at the Custom House. Meanwhile the rumor spread, of what was going on; and Judge BRANDEGEE, of the Police Court, hearing of it, went to the Custom House, with a large number of prominent citizens; and, on inquiring if the negro was a prisoner, was told by the Collector that he had him in charge, as a United States Commissioner. The Judge then asked the negro if he wished to stay there or go free. The negro chose to go. "Go then," replied the Judge; and in spite of some attempts by the Custom House officials to prevent him, he *went.* Another fugitive from Wilmington has since escaped in the same way. Concealed on board a Boston brig, he had been two days out when he was found. The captain, like a law-abiding patriot, at once attempted to return; but the south-west wind prevented. He then bore up for Norfolk, Virginia; but, when within five miles of that port, was met by a gale from the north which drove him out to sea. The gale abating, he renewed the attempt, but head winds and a scarcity of provisions forced him at last to give it up and pursue his voyage. While coming up Boston harbor, the fugitive escaped at night to Lovell's Island, and before he was missed had hailed a passing sloop, which took him to the city, where he arrived, a freeman,

on the 26th day of December. News that a Slave was on the
brig preceded him, and steps to rescue him were promptly taken.
Judge Russell issued a writ of habeas corpus, and with the
sheriff and his posse, went down the harbor and boarded the
brig; but found that the man had already served his own original writ, and taken his body into his own keeping.

Less fortunate was a poor fellow who attempted to escape in
like manner from Mobile, last August. He was discovered
when only a day or two out, and was immediately carried back.
The Mobile *Register* was touched with a lively sense of the
merit of the worthy captain, Samuel G. Fairchild, who,
"whether or not he will receive that reward which is due him
from all Slaveholders, has still the satisfaction of feeling that he
has done all his duty, and *even more;* for instead of landing
the negro at some southern port, convenient on his route, which
is all the law requires, he returned to the port whence the fugitive attempted to escape." Sweet is the sense of duty done!—
how doubly sweet the consciousness of meritorious works of
supererogation! "O, thrice, yea, four times happy," Captain
Fairchild! If Mobile dollars pay not thy most generous self-
sacrifice in bearing back the bondman to his chains, still shall
the dulcet voice of an approving conscience cheer thee; and in
thy silent musings thou shalt hear, perhaps, another voice, in
accents clear, proclaiming, "inasmuch as thou hast done it unto
one of the least of these, my brethren, thou hast done it unto
me." Another instance of alacrity in the discharge of sacred,
constitutional obligations must not be left unnoticed. Two
Slaves, who had escaped to Canada, returned to Cincinnati,
about the end of August, to show some friends the road to
freedom. Betrayed by a colored man, whom they had trusted,
they were seized and dragged, at a late hour in the evening,
before Commissioner Newhall, who at first demurred to acting
at so late an hour, but yielded when the Slaveholder insisted on
his *rights;* performed his task with due celerity, and at mid-
night gave the prey into the spoiler's hand. But, after all, a
great lack of zeal among the northern people, generally, in this
Union-saving work of Slave-catching, must be inferred from
such infrequency of its performance, that, though we have
looked through the journals of the year past with some care,
we have found mentioned in them only ten or twelve cases of

actual reënslavement of fugitives who had reached a Northern
State. And the process seems expensive, when successful; for
we learn from a Virginia paper that it cost two thousand dollars
to get back a company of seven, last fall, though they were
taken within thirty miles of where they fled from. The
chances of success, moreover, in this kind of work, are not apparently improving.

A case was lately tried in Philadelphia, intensely interesting
and exciting in its progress, and eminently cheering in its termination. One Daniel Webster, claimed as a fugitive Slave from
Virginia, was arrested in Harrisburg, on Saturday morning,
April second, and conveyed to Philadelphia, where the friends
of freedom, informed by telegraph of the arrest, were taking
measures to contest the claim; engaging able counsel, and
making all the preparation for a stout defence which their brief
time and scanty knowledge of the case permitted. For counsel, they retained WM. S. PEIRCE, an ever-ready volunteer for
such a service; and GEORGE H. EARLE, whose bearing in the
trial proved that it was for no lack of good will to the work, if
this was his first essay in it; and EDWARD HOPPER, who, if ever
man had a legitimate inheritance, inherits a good title to the
championship of those in danger of enslavement. The captive,
manacled and guarded by the Marshal and his posse, arrived
early in the afternoon, when a friend, concerned in his defence,
was allowed to see and talk with him in presence of the officers,
but the privilege which a murderer, awaiting trial would have had,
of privately conferring with his counsel, was denied him. The
remonstrance of his friend, however, did avail to get his manacles
removed, and to draw from the Marshal a sort of 'gruff apology
for having put them on. He was soon after brought before Commissioner LONGSTRETH, and the claimant's counsel, BENJAMIN
H. BREWSTER, urged a "prompt and summary" disposal of the
case. The prisoner's counsel asked delay to give them time for
preparation, and because two of them were called away that afternoon, by previous engagements, and the third was unwilling
to proceed alone. After some debate, and an affirmation by the
prisoner's friend, J. M. McKIM, that word by telegraph from Harrisburg gave reason to expect important testimony by another
day, the Commissioner granted a continuance till Monday
morning. By that time all the city was aroused. The place of

trial was densely crowded, and not a hundredth part of those
who wished could gain admission.   The moral worth and best
respectability of Philadelphia were as fully represented as the
limitation of space allowed.   True-hearted men were there, and
noble women, not a few.   Bound by the force of generous feeling, and clear, strong sense of right, to give the righteous
cause what aid their presence and a show of lively sympathy
could give in its apparent peril; to cheer, with what encouragement they might, the drooping spirit of the seemingly doomed
victim of a wicked law.   The well-known Abolitionists of
Philadelphia and its neighborhood were there, of course, but
many more were with them there, in heart and soul, as well as
body.   LUCRETIA MOTT sat at the prisoner's side through all
the trial.   Among the sympathizers with him, was an aunt of
the Commissioner.   It was plain that if another victim must
be laid upon the Southern Moloch's altar, at least it should be
done before no mean array of witnesses, and with a sense of the
responsibility which such an act incurs to public sentiment, as
well as law.

Monday forenoon was spent in the reading of the claimant's
papers, and debating the objections of the prisoner's counsel,
who were watchful to detect and quick to expose every real or
apparent flaw, and succeeded in getting one document ruled
out.   The claimant alleged that Daniel had escaped in 1854;
and in the afternoon brought witnesses to prove this fact, and
the prisoner's identity.   These were all Virginians, and most of
them, as it came out on cross-examination, had some pecuniary
interest in the issue.   One was a member of the Baptist Church,
and thought he had "experienced a change of heart;" was
conscientious about swearing, so affirmed, instead; but as his
testimony showed, was not so scrupulous about lying; for when
Daniel was arrested he told the bystanders that it was for burg-
lary — fearing a rescue if the real cause were known.   The witnesses were positive as to both identity and the time of the
escape.   When the testimony closed, the afternoon being spent,
the prisoner's counsel asked for an adjournment.   BREWSTER objected, and again insisted on the claimant's right to a "summary"
proceeding; but the Commissioner adjourned to four o'clock
the next afternoon.   When that time came the scenes within
and around the Court room were the same as on the former

day.   After some time consumed in settling preliminary questions, the witnesses for the defence were called.   The first, an
aged, venerable-looking colored man, a minister in the Methodist Church, testified that he had known Daniel in Harrisburg,
in 1853, and had employed him in the digging of a cellar for a
house which he had built that year.   The dates in a receipt
book, which he presented, corroborated his testimony as to the
time.   He stood a severe cross-examination of two hours and a
half so admirably well, that even his examiner was constrained
to say that he believed him to be a truthful and conscientious
man.   The other witnesses confirmed his testimony, with added
circumstances.   Then the Commissioner, at EARLE's request,
measured the prisoner's height, and found it, when his boots
were on, five feet ten inches; and when they were off, five
feet, eight inches and nine-tenths.   The claimant's papers
described a man five feet seven or eight inches high.

The Commissioner announced that he would close the trial at
that sitting.   Some testimony was given to rebut that of one
of the prisoner's witnesses, but none which touched the statements of the first and most important.   At half-past twelve, a
brief recess was taken; then came the arguments of counsel,
filling up the time till after sunrise; BREWSTER consuming three
hours for the claimant, and EARLE and PEIRCE about one each
for the defence.   Both sides were ably argued; but on one it
was an able stating and applying of the letter of the law, regardless of its moral character; a shrewd defence of barbarism and
iniquity embodied in the statute; on the other, eloquence, and
logic, and legal acumen, were all informed with the warm life
of justice and humanity.   While EARLE and PEIRCE drew inspi-
ration from their cause, which rendered them its not unworthy
champions, BREWSTER could only earn the equivocal praise of
having "made the best of a bad cause."   Yes, one thing more
he earned — his fee of $200 — and worked cheaply at that,
taking into the account the wear and tear of manhood incident
to such a task.   The prisoner's counsel took the ampler com-
pensation of their voluntary labor, in coinage such as generous
hearts appreciate, but no mint scales weigh.   And now, the
conflict over, after a session of fourteen hours, from four
o'clock on Tuesday afternoon, throughout the whole of which
the prisoner's friends had been steadfast at their post, and none

12

with firmer constancy or more wakeful vigilance and untiring interest than the band of faithful women, all were relieved at six on Wednesday morning, by an adjournment to four in the afternoon, for the rendering of the decision. Meanwhile it was awaited with intense anxiety. One token of the widely prevalent feeling was exhibited at the mid-day revival prayer meeting, in Sansom street, in the suspension, for that day, of the interdict of "controverted topics," that prayer might be offered for the deliverance of Daniel. At four o'clock, the Court room and the street were thronged again. All, for a time, was silence and suspense, while the Commissioner was reading his opinion, and none dared hope for a favorable conclusion; but when the end began to be foreshadowed, and soon might be anticipated with scarce a doubt, hardly could the expression of intense feeling be kept down until the last words came ordering the prisoner to be discharged!—and then rolled out the jubilant acclaim, from full hearts, pouring forth full-voiced, peal after peal; a signal from an open window told the glad tidings to the crowded street, which answered with a roar of exultation; from street to street, from square to square, flashed the electric thrill, and all the city was alive with joy. The colored people called for Daniel, and as he came out a free man, they overwhelmed him with congratulations, placed him in a carriage standing near, removed the horses, and all who could get near enough laid hold and drew him down the street in triumph. So Daniel was delivered from the den. God's angels had gone in and shut the lions' mouths, and he walked out unhurt, in sight of the rejoicing multitudes.

On Friday evening, a large, enthusiastic and effective meeting, held in Sansom Hall, improved the occasion to promote the interests of the Anti-Slavery cause. A mob attempted to disturb the meeting, but was promptly put down by the police. Had anything been wanting to the completeness of Wednesday's victory, it was now supplied. For the first time, the Philadelphian authorities had put down a Pro-Slavery mob. The Philadelphia Female Anti-Slavery Society, which lets no event related to our cause go by without a proper pointing of its moral, at its next meeting, in the following week, unanimously adopted a preamble and resolutions, denouncing the late trial of a man on the charge of being a Fugitive Slave, as disgraceful to the city and an insult to the State; an outrage on humanity and a heinous sin against God; expressing joy at the deliverance of Daniel Webster, but regret that it was not because he is a man, but only because he was not identified with the Slave the claimant sought; commending the Commissioner's restoring him to freedom, but solemnly remonstrating against his permitting such a cause to be tried before him, and his holding an office which requires him to execute the infamous Fugitive Siave Act; thanking Messrs. Peirce, and Earle, and Hopper, who without pecuniary recompense had advocated the defendant's claim to liberty, with eminent ability and zeal, laboring with unwearied assiduity by day and by night in his behalf; alluding to the misconduct of the United States officers during the trial, and to the subsequent attempt of a mob to wrest the right of free speech from the citizens assembled in an Anti-Slavery meeting, as showing unmistakably the cowardice and fury of the Slave Power; and declaring that this attempt to kidnap a man "on our own soil," should arouse a determination to endeavor to procure the repeal of the Fugitive Slave Statute, and to obtain from the State Legislature the passage of a law forbidding that Pennsylvania shall be a hunting-ground for Slave-catchers.

RESCUES AND THEIR CONSEQUENCES.

On the 13th of last September, John Rice, a colored man, living at Oberlin, Ohio, was decoyed from the village on pretence that he was wanted by one Boynton, a farmer in the neighborhood, to dig potatoes. While riding out with Boynton's boy, the bearer of the message, he was met a mile or two from town, by two Slave-hunters, (who had hired the boy, for $20, to do their treacherous errand;) was hurried off to Wellington, the nearest station on the Cleveland and Columbus railroad, and confined in a tavern to await the next train for Columbus. When the alarm reached Oberlin, there was great excitement and an eager rush in pursuit. People along the road and in Wellington joined the pursuers; the tavern was surrounded, and a Justice of the Peace, with several assistants, went in to hold a parley with the kidnappers. They found the colored man in the keeping of a Deputy Marshal of the United States, named Lowe, and his assistant, DAVIS, and two Kentuckians, JENNINGS and MITCHELL, who claimed him as a runaway Slave of one BACON, of Kentucky. The Marshal showed a warrant from a United States Commissioner in Columbus, for the arrest of BACON's Slave; but as Commissioner and Marshal both were of the Southern District of Ohio, neither had any legal authority in Oberlin or Wellington, which are within the Northern District. JENNINGS had a power of Attorney from BACON, to take his Slave, but it does not appear that he exhibited it. After an hour or two of parley, the out-door crowd becoming impatient and clamorous, the Slave-hunters, fearing for themselves, gave up their captive, who was rapidly conveyed to parts unknown.

On the 6th of December, the Grand Jury of the United States District Court, sitting at Cleveland, indicted thirty-seven alleged participators in the rescue; a few of Wellington, but most of Oberlin. Among them were Professor PECK, of Oberlin College, several Theological students, and others of the most respectable citizens. The traitor, BOYNTON, was a member of the Grand Jury. On the morning of the 8th, obedient to a summons of Marshal JOHNSON, who had not thought it needful to arrest them, those of the indicted who reside in Oberlin went to Cleveland to appear in Court, cheered loudly at their departure by a crowd of men and women gathered at the station to show them sympathy. The Mayor and a number of the principal citizens volunteered to go with them, and see them comfortably quartered or safely returned. In Cleveland, too, they met expressions of warm sympathy and approval. Four able lawyers volunteered to defend them without charge,—Hon. R. P. SPAULDING, Hon. A. G. RIDDLE, S. O. GRISWOLD, and F. T. BACKUS; of whom the first is said to stand nearly or altogether at the head of the Cleveland bar, in age, experience, legal learning, and ability, and weight of personal and professional character. At 2 P. M. they were arraigned, and asked an immediate trial; but the prosecutor was not ready,—wished for time to send to Kentucky for witnesses. Judge Spaulding strenuously opposed delay, but a continuance was granted; and the prisoners, refusing to give bail, were discharged on their own recognizances to appear at the March Term. One of the accused, who, before the notice of his indictment came to Oberlin, had gone to take a school in Franklin County, was there arrested in the afternoon of January 14th, by the fellow, DAVIS, who was with LOWE at Wellington; was manacled, in presence of his pupils, though he told the ruffian he should make no resistance; thrown into the Columbus jail and kept there until 3 o'clock next morning, without food or opportunity — for which he asked — to communicate with his friends in the city; and then was taken to Cleveland, where the Judge at once discharged him on his own recognizance.

The trials were commenced on the 5th of April, beginning with the case of SIMEON BUSHNELL, driver of the wagon in which John rode off, after the rescue. From what the Oberlin *Evangelist* says of the composition of the jury, we gather that the Marshal who had summoned it had fully done his part towards a conviction. "Gathered from the northern half of Ohio, it exhibits, out of sixteen names on the panel, only one from the Reserve. Taken from a district which numbers tens of thousands of Anti-Slavery men, and which is, by an overwhelming majority, Republican in politics, it has, so far as we have ascertained, neither an Abolitionist nor a Republican on the list." If this result came not of careful culling, was ever chance so marvellous before? The opening of the case, and the hearing of testimony occupied six or seven days, and the arguments of counsel, about three. The District Attorney undertook to prove that John was BACON's Slave; that JENNINGS, and not LOWE, had him in charge, holding him under the valid power of attorney, not under the void warrant, and that the rescuers were informed of this, and therefore took him knowingly from legal custody. But the evidence failed to sustain his allegations. His witnesses testified to having shown their papers, but did not say *what* papers; while those to whom they were shown testified that the *only* paper exhibited to them was the warrant in LOWE's hands, that the power of attorney was not spoken of, and that LOWE, not JENNINGS, acted as John's keeper. A doubt of the validity of the power of attorney, too, was raised, because of informality in execution. Nor was the proof as to identity beyond a question. JENNINGS and MITCHELL swore, indeed, that John was the Slave referred to in the papers, but the power of attorney described a copper-colored man, five feet eight or ten inches high, weighing a hundred and sixty or a hundred and eighty pounds; and it was testified that

John was black, five feet four or five inches high, weighing a hundred and thirty or a hundred and forty pounds.

The counsel for the defence distinctly took the ground of "Higher Law," saying, "however men may sneer at it, they must submit to it or perish," and "no man who repudiates it can be a good citizen or an honest man." Judge SPAULDING argued that the Fugitive Slave Acts of Congress are unconstitutional; that the ruling of the present Supreme Court on certain questions touching Slavery is against all law and precedent, and the exorbitant power of that Court is dangerous to State and individual rights. He did not argue thus, he said, expecting to affect the Judge's ruling in this case but to show his own position, and to *agitate* till right is done. His clients were not alone in opposing the Fugitive Slave Law. Within a few years the District Attorney had sought his aid to get a nomination for Governor of Ohio, on the ground of opposition to this law. It was denounced as unconstitutional, tyrannical, and oppressive, and the fullest resistance to it was pledged, in resolutions unanimously adopted by a large, enthusiastic meeting held in Cleveland, in September, 1850. On the Committee which reported them, "was his Honor, now sitting as Judge of this Court."

The sympathy of the numerous spectators of the trial was evidently and strongly with the prisoners. RIDDLE was loudly applauded when he said, with hearty emphasis, that, law or no law, if the fugitive should come to him for succor and protection, he should have them to the fullest extent, so help him the living God! When the District Attorney threatened to commit the applauders if the demonstration were repeated, Judge SPAULDING promptly avowed and justified his own participation in it, and declared his readiness to meet the consequences.

In the forenoon of the 15th, the case was given to the jury with a charge, at the request of Mr. BACKUS, that, in order to convict, it was necessary to find it proved by the prosecution that John was held under the power of attorney, and not by the warrant. But the well-selected jury knew wherefore they were chosen; and in the afternoon brought in a verdict of "Guilty."

The case of CHARLES H. LANGSTON was next called; and it now came out that the Judge and District Attorney purposed to try all the cases by the same jury; which — as the main facts in all the cases were the same — had already, by its verdict, announced that its mind was made upon all the prominent points at issue. The prisoner's counsel protested against such a course, as an "unheard-of outrage," and "a mockery of justice." The Court persisting, SPAULDING said the accused would call no witnesses, and make no defence before such a jury. "Then," replied the District Attorney, "I ask the Court to order these men into the custody of the Marshal;"—which was immediately done. At the demand of their counsel, their recognizances were then canceled, and the Court adjourned to Monday, the 18th. As the prisoners declined to give bail, or enter recognizances, or even accept the Marshal's offer to let them go home on their simple promise to return on Monday morning; saying, with thanks for his courtesy, that since the District Attorney had placed them in his custody, they would stay there till relieved in due course of law; they were at once conducted to the county jail. The sheriff, after consultation with the County Commissioners, consented to receive them, not as prisoners, but as guests, and gave them such accommodations as his sitting-room and chambers could afford.

On Monday the contest was renewed about the jury. Judge SPAULDING challenged the array, and after some time spent in the controversy, the Judge gave way and ordered a new jury, which the Marshal at once proceeded to empanel. From what we learn, it seems to have been as judiciously select as its predecessor.

While LANGSTON's trial was proceeding, measures were in progress to give the contest a new aspect. Judge SPAULDING, on the 21st, applied to the Supreme Court of Ohio for a writ of habeas corpus on the prisoners' behalf; claiming that the law is unconstitutional under which they are imprisoned, and that the State Court owes protection to the citizens of Ohio, against infringements of their liberty by the Federal Judiciary. The Court immediately granted a rule upon the Marshal, which was served the next day, to show cause why the writ should not issue. The Marshal was enraged, and openly declared that neither would he, nor should the Sheriff, ever take the prisoners to Columbus; but it was decided, on consultation of the Federal officials, that the District Attorney should appear before the

State Court, and oppose the issuing of the writ. Before the service of the rule, the Marshal had been told, by telegraph, that it was coming; and knowing that if a habeas corpus should be granted, the Sheriff would obey it with alacrity, he sought to get the prisoners back into his own hands. By trick and false pretence he succeeded with BUSHNELL, and kept him illegally confined in his own room, the Sheriff refusing to give up the mittimus on which the prisoner had been put into his keeping, and claiming him as legally his prisoner still.

On the 25th and 26th the application for the habeas corpus was argued at Columbus, and on the 28th the Court unanimously decided to refuse it, on the ground that as none of the prisoners had yet been sentenced, the cases were still pending in the United States Court, and it was not to be presumed, until an actual decision, that injustice would be done to the parties there. This left the question open still, whether the Court would grant the writ, if asked for, after sentence. Whether because the habeas corpus was refused, or fearing possible unpleasant consequences of his illegal procedure, the Marshal soon after restored BUSHNELL to the Sheriff. Meanwhile, the case acquired another complication. Shortly before the trials were commenced, the Grand Jury of Lorain County unanimously indicted JENNINGS, MITCHELL, LOWE, and DAVIS, for an attempt to kidnap JOHN RICE. LOWE was arrested on the fourth of April, while on his way to Cleveland, and was held to bail in $1000 to appear for trial in the Lorain Court, on the 17th of May. On the 22d of April, JENNINGS and MITCHELL being then in Cleveland to testify against the rescuers, the Deputy Sheriff of Lorain went thither with warrants to arrest them. To save them from arrest, the District Judge committed them to the Marshal's custody as witnesses, and they were locked up in his room in the intermissions of the sitting of the Court. On the 25th, the Marshal raised and swore in a posse of about one hundred deputies, to aid — it was suspected — in carrying out some plan for the escape of the Kentuckians. But, if such was his design, it was baffled by the vigilance of the Lorain Sheriff, who set a guard around the Federal building and kept watch upon it day and night, while a strong force was held in readiness to support the guard, if needful. On the fifth of May, the Marshal received a letter from Attorney General Black, directing him, in case the State Court should issue a writ of habeas corpus for the prisoners, "to resist it at all hazards, and by every means in his power." That night the United States war steamer Michigan came into the harbor of Cleveland with a force of 70 to 100 marines on board.

On the sixth of May, four of the rescuers, from Wellington, were persuaded by the Marshal to plead "guilty," and throw themselves on the mercy of the Court. The District Attorney apologized for them, that they had been misled by the Oberlin "Higher Law fanatics;" and they were sentenced to pay a fine of twenty dollars, and the costs, and be imprisoned twenty-four hours. The Oberlin men all stand firm, and show no signs of yielding. Large public meetings have been held at Oberlin and elsewhere, to cheer them with expressions of the warmest sympathy and heartiest approval, and to denounce the tyrannical and unjust conduct of the prosecution. The Oberlin meeting also resolved "that we will not forget the *families* of our friends, who have been called to suffer for their work of righteousness, and we tender them our sympathy, and will share with them our material supplies, while deprived of their natural providers." A Committee was appointed to inquire into the wants of all who were thus deprived.

The trial of Wm. M. Connelly, in the United States District Court, at Cincinnati, on the charge of harboring and secreting Fugitive Slaves, ended the 22d of last May in his being sentenced to ten dollars fine and twenty days imprisonment. While in prison he was visited by troops of friends, eager to show approval of what he had done. The members of the Unitarian Conference, then in session in Cincinnati, went in a body to see him, and to testify, as they did, in strong terms, their abhorrence of the law which had condemned him for a humane and Christian act. When his term expired, a torch-light procession of between two and three thousand Germans, with enthusiasm unabated by a drenching rain, escorted him from the jail to the Turners' Hall, where music and speeches filled up the hours of a festive evening. Not the least spicy part of the entertainment seems to have been Connelly's showing that the "crime" for which he had been punished, was but a following of instructions given by the prosecutor himself, ten years before. He read extracts from a paper edited, in 1847-8,

13

by the prosecuting Attorney, in which the duty of assisting Fugitive Slaves was urged.

On the 28th of May, a New York schooner, T. S. LOVELAND master, homeward bound from Isle of Wight, Va., was seized in the James River, by the authorities of Norfolk, for having a Fugitive Slave concealed on board; the Slave was sent back to bondage, and the captain and crew were thrown into prison to await examination. They were examined by the Court, in Isle of Wight county, on the 6th, 7th, and 8th of July; and proved, by testimony of "gentlemen of the highest standing," — so says the Norfolk *Argus,* all whose eyes were of course wide open to watch the trial, — that they were men of "exemplary character;" that is, not that they were honest, upright, generous, humane — it does not seem to have been thought needful to speak of qualities like these — but that they were notoriously Pro-Slavery; had, both North and South, defended "Southern rights" against the "Black Republicans," and "were ready to do so to the last extremity." The captain "had been often heard to say that if the Black Republicans should divide the Union, he would go South to live." This evidence, as it manifestly should, convinced the Court and everybody else that they had had no part in the dark chattel's criminal attempt to become a man. They were released on very moderate bail — $100 each — and would, the *Argus* thinks, have been at once acquitted, had the Court been sitting as a jury. But in this testimony and its consequences, one of the schooner's men was not included, — the black cook. After the trial of the whites, he was brought in and "made a full confession." He said he was only nineteen years of age, and hearing from the brother of the Slave how badly he was treated, his feelings were so wrought upon that he agreed to run him off to New York. Without the knowledge of another soul on board, he hid him in the forecastle. Whether the youth of the offender, or the unselfish motive of his act, or his honest frankness in exonerating his white companions, or all these considerations together moved the Court to unwonted clemency, the *Argus* does not say. It tells us only that "the black cook was sent to the penitentiary for ten years." Subsequently the captain and white crew were acquitted, but the vessel was condemned and sold.

On the 6th of last June, WM. B. BAYLIS, of Wilming-

ton, Delaware, sailed on his homeward voyage from Petersburg, Virginia, in a small schooner of which he was master.
Five Slaves being missed in Petersburg on the same day, BAY-
LIS was suspected of having helped them off. The next day, a
party with an officer and a search warrant followed, on a steamboat; overtook and boarded the schooner, and by a strict search
found all the missing Slaves; put them and Capt. BAYLIS and
his mate — who made up his whole crew — on board the steamboat; then took the schooner in tow and returned to Petersburg. A dense and highly excited crowd met them at the
landing, and greeted the captives with fierce outcries of vindic-
tive rage. Hardly could the Mayor and police protect them
from the popular fury till they were lodged in jail. The Slaves,
whose voyage towards freedom had ended so disastrously, were
at once surrendered to their masters. One of them said that he
was on his way to join his wife in New York, whither she had
previously escaped. Another had already engaged a situation
as a waiter in a hotel in Canada. Capt. BAYLIS was tried on the
10th, before the Circuit Court, convicted on five separate counts,
one for each Slave he had tried to rescue, and sentenced to eight
years' imprisonment for each, or forty years in all; in effect, to
imprisonment for life. His wife is virtually made a widow, and
his children fatherless. The grave has swallowed him alive.
And this is what Slaveholding legislators and Slaveholding
judges call justice! The London *Daily News*, commenting on
this sentence, says, "whenever Americans assemble on the 4th
of July, or any other day, it must surely be felt as a national
disgrace and misfortune that any of their group of republics
should in this age resort to severities of punishment, for a con-
ventional offence, for which the most retrograde State in Europe
would be despised and reprobated." The mate was afterwards
acquitted and discharged, as it appeared that he knew nothing
of the attempted escapes, until the search revealed the fugitives.

Near the end of July, HUGH HAZELETT, of Dorchester
County, Maryland, was arrested in Caroline County, with seven
Slaves who had escaped from Dorchester a week before. They
were all brought to Cambridge, where, as the Cambridge *Democrat* informs us, the large and indignant crowd assembled at
the news of their arrival, "with great forbearance" kept itself
"from lynching HAZELETT on the spot;" and he was taken to the

jail "and there *chained to the floor*, to wait until it shall be seen what course the law will take in the case." WILLIAM BRODIE, a colored seaman from New York, convicted in Darien, Georgia, of helping Slaves to escape, was sold, last fall, into Slavery for sixty-five years, for the amount of fine and costs imposed upon him. Three free colored men, convicted in the Circuit Court of Frederick County, Maryland, a few weeks later, were sentenced to be sold out of the State, as Slaves for life. About the latter part of November, RICHARD CALE, a free colored man living near Port Penn, Delaware, convicted of aiding the escape of a Slave woman, was sentenced to be whipped, to pay the cost of prosecution, and to be sold for seven years within or out of the State.

When JOHN G. FEE, of Kentucky, became an Anti-Slavery man, he purchased of his father the woman who had nursed him in his infancy, and set her free. For four years past she has lived in Clermont County, Ohio; but several of her children — born before her liberation — and her grandchildren are still Slaves in Kentucky. For attempting to rescue them from Slavery, she was arrested on the 18th of October last, in Bracken County, Kentucky, and kept in the county jail until the 3d of March; when she was brought to trial. The jury, after being out but twenty minutes, pronounced her guilty; and she was sentenced to three years in the penitentiary. Such is Kentucky law, for the woman who asserts her claim to her own offspring. A free colored man in Washington, the husband of a Slave woman, and whose children are consequently Slaves, was imprisoned in that city — the nation's capital — about the first of February, on a charge of having harbored his own son, reared by himself while the mother was at work for her master. The boy, having become old enough to earn money for his "owner," whom he has cost not even the expense of "raising," was put out to service — the receiver of his wages never thinking, we presume, how unutterably *mean* is such a picking of the pockets of industrious poverty — but awhile after, it is said, went back for a few days to his father, who is accused of having actually fed and sheltered him. For this crime he is held to answer, having been released, on bail, in the sum of $2000.

SOUTHERN LAWLESSNESS AND BARBARISM.

The last year, like its predecessors, has brought us frequent
revelations of the barbarizing influence of the "peculiar system;"
and of its tendency to practically annul all law which is not the
instrument of its own wickedness, the guarantee of its assumed
"rights," or at least the tacit confessor of its supremacy. A few
of these we notice.

Rev. J. A. Todd, minister of the Dutch Reformed Church in
Tarrytown, N. Y., in a letter to the New York *Tribune*, published nearly a year ago, relates some incidents of an excursion in
the South from which he had then recently returned. Mr. Todd
is not an Anti-Slavery agitator. Though he "has no sympathy
with Slavery," and "hopes that a wise Providence will furnish
means to bring it to an end," yet he disapproves the doctrines
and measures of Northern Abolitionists, and has "always opposed the introduction of the Slavery discussion into the Tract
Society." Thus he expressed himself at the South, but not ob-
trusively, only in courteous response to the direct questioning of
Southern men, in private and familiar conversation. But all
his moderation of opinion and gentlemanly demeanor did not
save him from repeated insult, or hinder him from reaching the
conclusion, by his "own experience and observation," that, on
the Southern seaboard, "the negroes and the whites, so far as relates to the enjoyment of free speech, are all Slaves together."
In Augusta, Ga., some civil answers, which he made to questions put to him, raised such a stir that a Committee of the
citizens was appointed to inform him that he "must not express
any more such sentiments while in that city." At Charlotte,
N. C., while conversing one afternoon with two men who had
invited him to their office, he dissented, in reply to one of them,
from the doctrine that the Bible sanctions Slavery; when the
other, a Presbyterian deacon, too, rudely commanded him to
leave the office. In the evening he was waited on, first by the
Marshal of the place, sent, as he said, by the authorities and
citizens; then by a mob of thirty or forty persons; and told
that he must leave Charlotte in the train which would pass at
half past one, that night. He had intended to go by a train
four hours later, and adhered to that intention. In the parley

he was told that nothing would be allowed to be said there against Slavery, even in private.

In the excitement caused by the discovery of a Slave on LOVELAND'S schooner, the citizens of Norfolk drove from that city Capt. WILLETT MOTT and WM. DANNENBURG, and ordered the removal thence of two colored men, EDMUND WHITE and GEORGE WASHINGTON, on suspicion, or pretence of suspicion, that they had helped the escape of Slaves. MOTT sent his wife and children to New York, but went himself to Richmond, to take advice of counsel. After nearly five months spent in vain endeavors to procure a guarantee of protection, now from the authorities of Norfolk, and now from the Governor of the State, — offering to abide a trial, either judicial or by a Committee of citizens,— he ventured, on the 13th of October, to return to Norfolk, hoping to be allowed to stay and take care of his abandoned property. But before the day had passed, the signs of purposed violence became so manifest, that he yielded to the urgent counsels of his friends, fled from the city, and joined his family in New York.

JAMES L. BOWERS, a worthy Anti-Slavery man and peaceable "Friend," living in Kent County, Md., was decoyed from his house, late at night, on the 23d of June, by a call for help from a man pretending to have broken his carriage; was seized as he came into the road, by a gang of ruffians, taken to the woods half a mile distant, stripped and tarred and feathered, and commanded to leave the State in twenty-four hours. His wife, who hastened to his aid on hearing his outcry, was repelled with violence and insult while endeavoring to save him; though her condition should have shielded her from the rudeness even of ruffianism itself. The gang then finished their night's work by tarring and feathering a poor, old, dwarfish, wayfaring colored woman, "scarcely weighing fifty pounds," — says the Maryland paper which records the chivalrous exploit, with evident approval, — and severely flogging a free negro in whose house they found her. The potent reason for this display of Southern manliness was that the old woman "leads a migratory life," and "her advent has been followed" more than once "by the escape of Slaves."

Instead of obeying the command to leave the State, Mr. BOWERS went to Chestertown, the county seat, and lodged complaint against the authors of the outrage, and was put under bonds to appear and testify at the October Term. At the call of the State's Attorney, who assured him of protection, he returned, on the 14th of October, to the neighborhood whence he had been driven, to attend to the prosecution of his complaint. The Slaveholders, hearing of it, held a conclave at the county seat, and conspired to take him from the county before the sitting of the Court, which was to begin on the 18th. That day, at early dawn, a mob of more than thirty, armed with guns and pistols, and led by a member of Congress, J. B. RICAUD, surrounded his sister's house, where he was stopping with his wife, who had given birth to a child two days before. Though told of her feeble state, the mob prepared to force an entrance, and threatened to tear down the house unless he would come out. Under solemn promises of protection he consented to go with them, and was taken to the nearest railroad station, guarded by the Congressman and seven of his associates, fully armed, and put on board a train for Wilmington, Del., whence he went to Philadelphia.

In the fall of 1857, an old man named BELL, and his son, were kidnapped in Harrison County, Ia., and taken to Brandenburg, Kentucky, and there arrested on a warrant, charged with having secreted runaway Slaves. They lay in prison nine or ten months, waiting the convenience of their captors to bring them to trial. A Colonel MARSH, of Harrison County, who had interested himself to procure their release on bail, was shot down in the street of Brandenburg, and his murderer permitted to escape. Last summer, two sons of BELL, HORACE and JOHN, returned from California; and one day about the first of August, when the jailor of Brandenburg and most of the citizens were absent at a barbecue, entered the town at mid-day, obtained the keys of the prison from the jailor's wife, released their father and brother, and took them home in safety. The citizens of Brandenburg offered a large reward for the rescuers. On the 23d of October, HORACE BELL was called, by some occasion, to New Albany, Ia., while the citizens were mostly out of town attending the County Fair; when he was set upon by five or six men from Louisville, Ky., dragged to the ferry-boat, which was in waiting — the few who saw the assault being told he was arrested for murder — and hurried to Kentucky. There he was manacled, conveyed to Brandenburg, and thence, for fear of a rescue, to some place of confinement further from the river. The people of the Indiana shore, highly excited, took energetic measures for his liberation. A steamboat from New Albany, with a large armed party and a swivel on board, anchored before Brandenburg on the 28th, and a delegation went on shore to hold a parley. A meeting of the citizens was called, and a Committee chosen to confer with the Indianians, who threatened to blow up the jail unless satisfactory terms were made. It was at last agreed that BELL should be released on nominal bail, to be given by citizens of Brandenburg, and that the Governor of the State should be petitioned to quash all proceedings against the BELLS. The next day, BELL returned to New Albany, and was welcomed with much enthusiasm.

Dr. FRANCIS LIEBER, the well-known editor of the American Encyclopedia, and for a long time Professor of Political Economy and Moral Science in a South Carolina College, was driven from South Carolina, last summer, on account of an Anti-Slavery article which he published fifteen or twenty years ago, in the Encyclopedia. Last fall, SAMUEL GARBER, a minister of the the Dunker denomination, being on a visit to his friends in East Tennessee, accepted an invitation to preach there, and in his sermon incidentally alluded to Slavery as coming under the head of oppression, but said it was a subject on which he did not feel at liberty to speak. He was arrested and fined $234, though the church to which the sermon was preached unanimously testified that he did not preach specially against Slavery. The Richmond *South* mentions the imprisonment of a man named CRAWFORD, living in Prince William County, Va., in the early part of last winter, accused of having avowed himself an Abolitionist, said that a negro, who behaved well, was as good as he, and denied the right of property in Slaves. A lady from Brooklyn, N. Y., spending the winter in Aiken, S. C., in company with a sick daughter who required a mild climate, spoke, in a letter to her brother at the North, of the evils of Slavery, as she saw them. The letter was published, and a copy somehow reached Aiken. The citizens met and chose a committee to discover the writer. To save from threatened violence a gentleman who was suspected, the lady avowed the authorship, but said she was not privy to the publication. She

was peremptorily commanded to leave the place in forty-eight
hours. In vain she pleaded for more time on account of her
sick daughter, or to obtain the escort of her husband. The
landlord of the hotel was harsher still. He ordered her and her
sick child to leave his house in half an hour. How they accomplished their departure from among the savages we do not
learn, but, a few days after, her husband having heard by letter,
of their situation, met them at Columbia, on their homeward
way. A Mr. HAZARD, of Providence, R. I., described as an amiable, quiet man, and an invalid withal, was rudely assaulted by
the notorious Slave Trader, LAMAR, threatened with tar and
feathers, and driven from Savannah, Ga., a few weeks ago, upon
the allegation, whether true or false we know not, that he had
written to a Rhode Island paper an account of the sale of the
Wanderer, containing what LAMAR pronounced false statements. THOMAS B. YOUNG, "an estimable gentleman," of Philadelphia, eminently "conservative" on the Slave question, was
lately sent to Mississippi to arrest a citizen of Holly Springs, in
that State, who had defrauded certain Philadelphia merchants
of several thousand dollars. Armed with the proper papers, a
requisition from the Governor of Mississippi being one, he
reached the place in the latter part of March, and took the
man; but the people in a body refused to give him up, and
with threats of violence compelled the messenger to burn his
papers in their presence, and give a bond to leave the State
immediately, and never to return. The reason they alleged for
this procedure, was — unfortunately a lie — that Philadelphia
refuses to surrender Fugitive Slaves. Not far from the same
time, one CARTER, who by false pretences had obtained a quan-
tity of goods from a Philadelphia firm, was arrested in Alabama, by an officer sent from Pennsylvania, and was taken to
Huntsville. There the mob rose and rescued him, with furious
threats, defying all resistance; and, the next day, drove from
Huntsville the only man who had interfered to protect the
officer. The provocation, in this case, was the attempt to punish SHAW, in Pittsburg, for kidnapping FERRIS, claimed as a runaway Slave from Alabama.

On the 11th of March, the Arkansas Conference of the
Methodist Episcopal Church North met, according to appointment, at Bonham, the County seat of Fannin County, Texas.

14

This roused the ire of the Slaveholders in that region; for though the Methodist Church North is far enough from a right position as to Slavery, yet, as it does not explicitly concede the rightfulness of the system, but still has in its discipline a portion, much diluted, of the testimony borne by early Methodism against "the sum of all villanies," the morbid sensitiveness of Pro-Slavery ultraism sees in it only peril and annoyance. So, on the 12th, the citizens of Fannin met; a formidable array of titled dignitaries, judicial, military, and ecclesiastical, lending what dignity and weight long-handled names could lend to the assemblage. Speeches were made, and resolutions unanimously adopted, denouncing the Methodist Church North as "a secret foe," and its ministers as emissaries of Northern Abolitionists; declaring that their preaching must be stopped, peaceably or by force; proposing "to memorialize the Legislature" for "a law to punish the utterance of such seditious sentiments" as they hold; warning the Bishop and ministers that the continuance of their Conference would endanger the peace of the community, and pledging the meeting "to suffer no public expression of Abolition doctrines in that county to go unpunished." A Committee of fifty was appointed to wait on the Conference the next day — Sunday — read the resolutions, and "order the discontinuance of their meetings in this county henceforth and forever." At the head of this Committee was a judge who "was never in favor of mob law," but thought it "necessary that the people should take some decisive measure." On Sunday morning the mob Committee went to do its office. Entering the place of worship as the Bishop was about to begin his sermon, it made known, through its judicial chairman, the purport of the resolutions. After some parley and some threatening, the Bishop was permitted to conclude the services already begun; but was told that thereafter no meetings of his associates would be tolerated in that region. After the sermon, the Conference considered what should be done. It was decided that the members would at once return to their several stations and circuits, and abide by the decision of their people. If the people should say, "stay and preach," then they would do so; if otherwise, they would yield.

Among the items of news scattered through the papers of the past year, we find mention of the murder of several Slaves by their masters, mistresses, or other white persons, generally with circumstances of aggravated cruelty; or of trials for such murders, committed in former years; but in no instance have we seen an account of the punishment of the murderer. In some cases, the accused were still awaiting trial; in others, trial had resulted in acquittal, directly in the face of clear and convincing evidence. One of this latter class was that of three men, tried in Gates county, N. C., about the middle of October, for the horribly cruel killing of a Slave in the preceding August. The narrator of the case, a correspondent of the New York *Tribune*, writing from the place of trial, says: "not a year passes without some cases of this nature within this State." Another was tried at Fayetteville, N. C., in November, for a similar murder, in which three or four white men were concerned, a year and a half before. But yet more striking exhibitions of the prevalent barbarism of the Slave land, are given in instances from time to time occurring, of the public burning alive of Slaves guilty or suspected of such crimes as, when committed *upon* Slaves, go often if not always, wholly unpunished, though worthy of the penalties which civilized justice sanctions. Two cases of this kind have come to our knowledge within the year. In one of these, related by the Union Springs (Ala.) *Gazette*, of December 23d, a Slave who had murdered his master was doomed, by the unanimous vote of a public meeting of the citizens, to be burned alive; and, in the afternoon of the same day, was burned, in the presence of five hundred persons. The other case occurred at Troy, Ky., and is told by a correspondent of the Maysville, (Ky.) *Eagle*. On the 1st of January, when the annual negro sales had drawn a crowd together, eight hundred or a thousand persons, instigated by JAMES CALAWAY, whose brother-in-law had been murdered by his Slave a few days before, went to the jail, took out the murderer, and burned him to death in the jail-yard.

ACTION OF STATES.

The Legislature of Connecticut, at its last session, nearly a year ago, initiated an amendment to the State Constitution, to give to colored men the right of suffrage in that State. The vote in its favor in the House of Representatives was 112 to 94. To become a part of the Constitution, it must be approved by two-thirds of each House of this year's Legislature, and then must be adopted by a majority of the popular vote.

Last fall, the Legislature of Vermont, in answer to numerous petitions from the people, passed, by decided majorities in both Houses, "An Act to secure freedom to all persons in this State." It provides that "no person within this State shall be considered as property, or subject, as such, to sale, purchase, or delivery, or be deprived of liberty without due process of law;" that by due process of law is meant "the usual process issued by the Courts" of the State; that if any person shall be arrested on the ground that he owes service or labor to one not an inhabitant of the State, either party may claim a trial by jury; that the penalty for depriving or attempting to deprive a person of liberty, contrary to the Act, shall be a fine of not more than $2000 nor less than $500, and imprisonment not exceeding ten years; that descent from an African, Slave or free, or color of the skin shall disqualify no person for being a citizen of the State; that every person who has been held as a Slave, and who shall come to or be in the State, with or without the master's consent, or involuntarily, *or in any way, shall be* FREE; and whoever shall hold or attempt to hold such person, or any free person, as a Slave for any time, however short, under pretence that such person is or has been a Slave, shall be imprisoned not less than one year nor more than fifteen, and be fined not more than $2000.

The Legislature of Michigan, last winter, passed an Act — the vote upon it in the House of Representatives being 49 to 27 — prohibiting, on pain of imprisonment not more than ten years, and fine not over $1000, the bringing of a colored person into the State, claiming him as a Slave. In the House of Representatives, an amendment to the Constitution, striking out the word "white" from the article prescribing the qualifications of voters, was proposed by a Select Committee; but was indefinitely postponed by 39 to 31.

Petitions, numerously signed, asking for the enactment of a law against Slave-hunting, were sent to the Legislatures of Vermont, Massachusetts, New York, Pennsylvania, and Ohio, and perhaps some other States. The answer of Vermont we have already given. The petitions in Ohio were referred to a Committee of the House of Representatives, which reported that their prayer could not be granted without "a palpable violation" of "that ever-to-be-revered instrument," the Constitution of the United States; that "the rendition of 'fugitives from labor' is a solemn obligation imposed by the sacred compact of the Union;" that "the offering of such petitions indicates an unhealthy and rebellious public sentiment,"—recommended that in future such petitions be laid on the table without comment; and proposed, as a response to these, a resolution that "the General Assembly, as representatives of the loyal sentiment of the people of Ohio, are forever opposed to sectional and unconstitutional legislation, and deprecate in future all memorials praying for such enactments." The House adopted the resolution by 60 to 17.

The Massachusetts petitions, bearing more than sixteen thousand names, were referred, in the House of Representatives, to the Committee on Federal Relations; which reported, on the 11th of March, a bill, providing first, that no person now in the Commonwealth, or who may hereafter come, or be brought into it, shall be considered or treated as property; and second, that whoever shall arrest, imprison, or carry out of the Commonwealth, or attempt to do so, any person for the alleged reason that such person owes service or labor, as a Slave, to the party claiming him, shall be imprisoned in the State prison not exceeding five years. On the 28th and 29th of March, the bill was debated, ably and at much length; and on the 30th, the vote was taken. An amendment, offered by Mr. WELLS, of Greenfield, making the bill comparatively tame and pointless, was rejected by 132 to 84. An amendment, moved by Mr. GRIFFIN, of Malden, was adopted by 124 to 90. For the two sections of the original bill it substituted three; the first, substantially the original first; the second, expressly referring to the Fugitive Slave Acts of 1793 and 1850, and making any attempt to execute them, in the Commonwealth, punishable with imprisonment not less than three nor more than twenty years; and the third, in substance the original second, save that it in terms excepted from its operation all acts done under the two statutes just referred to, and made the penalty for violating it, imprisonment for life or not less than ten years. The bill, as thus amended, was then rejected by 109 to 106; two or three prominent Republicans, who had been at first regarded as friendly to the measure, voting now against it, contrary, we believe, to the decided wish and expectation of most of their constituents. They spoke "brave words" for freedom in the debate; but shrunk from bravely backing them when the ayes and noes were called; although conceding that the *thing* sought, Massachusetts means to have, after *some* fashion, if not this. One of them, Mr. WELLS, of Greenfield, said, "the sentiment of Massachusetts undoubtedly is, that *no Slave shall be carried out of her borders.*" Nor did he find fault with that sentiment; but he "would rather *act* treason than *enact* it." It is to be hoped that Massachusetts may some day be blessed with legislators bold and frank enough to *enact* all the treason which they mean to *act.*

In the New York House of Representatives, the petitions were referred to a select Committee, which, on the 26th of February, reported a bill containing all the provisions of the Vermont law, with much severer penalties; and, in addition, empowering any person, injured by a violation of its provisions, to sue for and recover damages in any Court of record in the State; forbidding any State officer to issue or serve any process or grant any certificate under the Fugitive Slave Bill, and any person to act as attorney or counsel for a Slave hunter; imposing a heavy penalty on any sheriff, constable, or policeman aiding to arrest, detain, or return a Fugitive Slave; and requiring the Governor, with advice of the Senate, to appoint in each county an attorney to defend all persons claimed as Fugitive Slaves. By a vote of 65 to 28, the bill was made the special order for the 2d of March; on the 30th, the prohibition of acting as attorney for a Slave-hunter being first struck out, it was ordered to a third reading, by 55 to 16; but on the 5th of April, when the vote was taken on its final passage, it was lost for want of a two-thirds majority — ayes 55, nays 44. The next day a reconsideration was moved and carried, by 80 to 21; the bill was recommitted to the Committee which reported it; and on the 8th, it was again reported to the House, so modified as to secure the necessary majority. It passed, that evening, by 84 to 22, shorn of a portion of its strength, but strong enough to make Slave-catching difficult, if not impossible, in New York, had it become a law; and too strong to go through the Senate, in the short time then remaining of the session. Before it went up from the House, the unamended bill had been presented in the Senate, referred to the Judiciary Committee, and — April 8th — reported on unfavorably; the Committee holding the Fugitive Slave Act to be binding on the people of New York, and arguing for obedience to it in the customary style of Northern, Union-saving Pro-Slavery politicians. One member dissented from the arguments of the majority, but concurred in the conclusion that the bill ought not to pass. Next day, the bill passed by the House, was sent up. As the presiding officer was about to hand it over to the Judiciary Committee, a reference to a Select Committee was moved, and carried by 11 to 10; and afterward, on reconsideration, carried again by 13 to 12. The enemies of the bill regarded this — and probably aright — as meant for a rebuke to the Judiciary Committee, for their report upon the Senate bill. The session closed a few days after, without final action on the question of concurrence.

On the 4th of April, a bill to authorize Ontario County to lease a portion of her Court House to the United States, being before the House, a motion to forbid its being used for the trial of Fugitive Slave cases was defeated by 52 to 35, and the bill was passed by 67 to 24. The House, on the 16th of March, by 83 to 21, and the Senate on the 6th of April, by 18 to 12, adopted a resolution so to amend the Constitution of the State, as to abolish the property qualification required of colored voters. The resolution must pass another Legislature, and be ratified by a vote of the people to become a portion of the Constitution.

In Pennsylvania, a not very stringent bill "for the better protection of persons claimed as Fugitive Slaves" was brought into the Legislature, but we do not learn that any decisive action was taken on it.

Last summer, Wisconsin gave another judicial response to the despotic assumptions of the Federal Courts. The State Circuit Court, by judgment in favor of Sherman M. Booth, in two replevin suits, restored to him the property which had been taken from him to satisfy a judgment of the United States District Court, in an action for damages on behalf of the pretended owner of Glover, rescued at Milwaukie, five years ago. More recently she has spoken with decided emphasis, both in the Legislative hall and at the polls, in confirmation of her position taken in 1854. The Supreme Court of Wisconsin, having denied the right of the Supreme Court of the United States to rejudge its decision in the Booth case, and having refused to certify a copy of its proceedings to that Court, to be examined by it, the latter surreptitiously obtained a copy of the record, and thereupon proceeded, as if the case had regularly come before it, to set aside the judgment of the Wisconsin Court; to reäffirm the constitutionality of the Fugitive Slave Act; and to deny the power of a State Court, either upon a writ of habeas corpus or upon any other process, to inquire into the validity of the process by which an officer of the United States holds a person in custody, or into the constitutionality of the Act under which the process issues. On hearing of this action of the Federal Court, the Legislature of Wisconsin, by 47 to 37 in the House of Representatives, and by 13 to 12 in the Senate, adopted resolutions declaring the "assumption of jurisdiction by the Federal Judiciary in the case before mentioned, an arbitrary act of power, unauthorized by the Constitution, virtually superseding the benefit of the writ of habeas corpus, and therefore void; that the government formed by the Constitution of the United States was not made exclusive judge of the extent of its delegated powers, but that, as in all cases of compact among parties having no common judge, each party has an equal right to judge both of infractions and of measures of redress; that the principle contended for by the ruling party in the nation, that the general government is exclusive judge of the extent of its own powers, is despotism; that the several States have a right to judge of infractions of the Constitution; and that a *positive defiance*, by those sovereignties, of all unauthorized acts done or attempted under cover of the instrument, is the right remedy." An election just then pending, to fill a vacancy in the Supreme Court of the State, gave to the people an opportunity to pass their judgment on the action of the Courts and Legislature. The issue was distinctly made between the opposing claims and doctrines of the State and Federal Courts; and, to give greater emphasis to their acceptance of that issue, the candidate selected by the supporters of the former was BYRON PAYNE, BOOTH's counsel in the Rescue trials. His argument before the Supreme Court of the State was one of the electioneering documents of his party, and it was clearly understood that his election or defeat was the approval or rejection of its doctrines by the people. The election took place on the 5th of April, and PAINE was chosen to the vacant seat, by a majority of eight or ten thousand votes. So Wisconsin speaks, in language unmistakable, her purpose to resist the usurpation of the Federal Courts, and protect her citizens against the petty tyranny of Federal officials. In this repudiation of the arrogant claims put forth at Washington by the judicial servants of the Slave Power, she has, if we mistake not, law as well as justice, and the principles of true Democracy upon her side. For it has always been conceded on all hands that the jurisdiction of the Federal Courts is special, limited to certain enumerated cases; the *residuum* of judicial power belonging to the States, whose courts are tribunals of general jurisdiction. Now the well-established legal doctrine we understand to be, that Courts of special jurisdiction are not the judges, in the last resort, of the limits of their own power. If either, then, is such, exclusively, it is the State Court. And manifestly it would be much safer for the people's rights to place the authority there, nearer themselves, and so less likely to be used against them, and where abuse could be more easily reached and corrected; while also it would have a less extensive range of mischief, and would be counterbalanced, in some measure, by the moral weight of other State tribunals, — than to confer it on the Federal Court, to be the engine of a Central despotism, empowered to crush, at its unlimited discretion, the freedom of the people and the independence of the States into one indiscriminate mass of hopeless, helpless vassalage.

In Missouri, the "irrepressible conflict" still goes on, apparently with varying success, but, as the Emancipationists affirm, with, on the whole, a steady progress of the Free Labor movement. It is resisted strenuously, however. On the 31st of January, the House of Representatives, by 83 to 15, voted to repeal the law prohibiting the importation of Slaves into that State. The repeal was moved and advocated expressly on the ground that it would reduce the price of labor. On the 9th of March, the House adopted, 88 to 29, the bill, to which we have before alluded, to drive out or enslave the free colored people, and all

15

who shall hereafter become free. Neither bill has passed the Senate. The St. Louis *Democrat* thinks that the action of the House upon the former of these measures will rouse the free white workingmen throughout the State against the friends of Slavery. But it is for the interest of the free *white* man, not for freedom as a principle, or for the rights of man, as man, that the Emancipation party generally appear to be contending. A Missourian correspondent of the New York *Tribune* says, "the *moral* sentiment against Slavery is not appealed to by the Free Democracy, nor would its aid be accepted. * * * * * They would not purchase emancipation at the price of permitting the negro to remain in Missouri. He must be deported hence or remain in Slavery. Hence that unconquerable spirit of Anti-Slavery enthusiasm which might, perhaps, be aroused in their favor, is idle here, and unsympathizing, or sympathizes only under protest. * * * * * There is a distinctive *Anti-Slavery* sentiment in St. Louis, and some of the candidates of the Free Democracy have injured their cause by *cowardly* allusions to the negro race." The writer holds a sound philosophy, in holding that the Emancipation cause would win a speedier, more complete success, if it would endeavor to enlist "the moral sentiment against Slavery;" appealing "to the nobler instincts of the people," than it can achieve by its present policy. "The Anti-Slavery sentiment," he says, "has a very thin crust over it, and the sooner it is removed, the more speedily — in spite of their unbelief — will the Free State Democracy establish their power on an impregnable basis." At the Congressional election on the 2d of August, FRANCIS P. BLAIR, the candidate of the Emancipation party in the St. Louis District, was defeated; but only, it was confidently believed, by means of extensive frauds, because of which he has announced his purpose to contest the seat, when Congress comes together. The suspicion of fraud was confirmed by the result of the St. Louis municipal election on the 4th of April, when the Free Labor party triumphed by a plurality of about three thousand votes; enough, says the St. Louis *Democrat*, to "satisfy every desire of the present, dispel every apprehension of the future, and at one magnanimously for the untoward event of August."

The Legislature of Florida took, last winter, what Pro-Slavery ultraism must regard as a step backward, by repealing the law which subjected colored seamen, coming into any port of Florida, to imprisonment during the stay of the vessel to which they belong. But if this strange vagary seems to call in question the sound and constitutional doctrine that black men have no rights which white men are bound to respect, its evil influence, we may hope, will in a good degree be neutralized by a decision given, last fall, in the Chancery Court of Southern Alabama, making a new application of Judge Taney's Dred Scott law. A former citizen of Mobile, owning there a large amount of real estate, removed to Louisiana, and afterwards to France, and died not long ago in Paris, having conveyed his real estate in Alabama to his children, "within three degrees of African descent," born in Louisiana, and living now in Europe. Some persons, claiming to be his heirs at law, filed a bill to set aside the conveyance. The Chancellor decided that free negroes born out of the State are aliens, and cannot take lands by deed or conveyance in the State. So the children were robbed of their father's gift, without risk of penitentiary to the robbers.

The Church.

No essential change has been revealed during the past year, in the character and position of the American Church in regard to Slavery. We still have our old testimony to bear against it, that as a whole it is practically on the side of the oppressor. We have seen no specially noteworthy movement relating to the subject, in any of the great denominations, since our last Report, unless it is the action of the Methodist Episcopal Church South, at its General Conference, last May, in Nashville, Tennessee. It there conformed its law to its already well-known practice, by striking from its Discipline, by 140 votes to 8, the rule forbidding "the buying and selling of men, women, and children, with intention to enslave them." But the Methodist Church North does not conform its practice to its law, for while it still retains the rule, it also keeps, in both its membership and "local" ministry, not only holders, but buyers and sellers of human beings as property. From the testimony of ministers of that Church, who have lived and labored for years in that part of its territory which lies within the Slave States, the editor of the Northern *Independent* estimates at not less than 10,500 the number of Slaveholding members in four of the seven Slaveholding Conferences. In the other three, he says, "the number of Slaveholders is not large, because our membership is quite limited." He adds, "it is greatly to be feared that nearly all the members of our Church in the Slave States are Slaveholders. The extreme repugnance of the preachers and people there to all Anti-Slavery movements proves conclusively that our Church is overrun with Slaveholding. Slaveholding is not the exception, but the rule." Seven Conferences are wholly or in part within Slave States, and "if the evil were confined to these," the *Independent* says, "it would be well." But the residence of Slaveholders in all parts of the Free States "is fast reducing us to a homogeneous condition, and the distinction of Slaveholding and non-Slaveholding Conferences will soon cease altogether. We must be better or worse." One preacher who has spent the greater part of his life in one of the "Slaveholding Conferences," declared that "there is no difference between our laity and the laity of the Church South." This statement having been questioned, another preacher, who has labored in the same region, thus replies to the questioner. "Do members of the Methodist Episcopal Church South possess Slaves by gift, inheritance, and having them born unto them? So do members of the Methodist Episcopal Church. Does the South permit her members to purchase their colored sisters for breeders? So does the North. Do the laity of the Church purchase Slaves when they desire? sell them when convenience or necessity demands? or hire their service out when interest suggests? Do men of the South derive large resources from the latter source? So do the laity of the Methodist Episcopal Church North. Do Southern saints scourge their women Slaves with cruel scourging? So do the Northern. And when the poor Slave runs away, do they offer large rewards for their apprehension? and having apprehended them, do they sell them South? So do the members of the Methodist Episcopal Church." The Discipline, moreover, still contains a rule which pays unchristian deference to the wicked prejudice of an oppressing people. It reads thus: "Our colored preachers and official members shall have all the privileges which are usual to others in Quarterly Conferences, *where the usages of the country do not forbid it.*"

True, we are aware, an earnest effort still goes on, to rid the Chu :h of these abominations; and to the noble laborers in this work we would award due credit, and wish abundant success; but, till it is achieved, the very need and merit of their labor are the warrant for our condemnation of their Church.

The Presbyterian bodies have, for aught we know, continued to enjoy that "blessed calm," and "rest from agitation" within their sacred enclosures, the sweet foretaste of which we chronicled last year.

On the 15th of August last, the Rev. Dr. FULLER, widely known as the champion of Slavery in debate with Dr. WAYLAND several years ago, preached to the "respectable white persons" who alone are permitted to own pews in the Church (Baptist) of Rev. BARON STOW, in Boston. If Dr. FULLER had maintained in public argument his right to put the coat or horse of his reverend brother STOW to his own use without the owner's leave, would he have been invited to that pulpit? We learn from the *American Baptist* that, last fall, the Philadelphia Baptist Association rejected a very moderate Anti-Slavery resolution, offered by Rev. Dr. MALCOM, expressing "sympathy for our brethren and sisters in this land, who are not allowed to read God's word, or to enjoy the privileges of the conjugal and parental relations," and calling on "those who hold political power in those portions of our country" where the evil is, "to devise early measures for securing to every member of the community the full privileges of Christianity."

Of the position of the Congregational Churches, and indeed of the so-called evangelical Churches generally, such facts as these are not without significance. While the boldness and vigor of Dr. CHEEVER's assaults upon Slavery, and his scathing rebukes of the complicity of Mission Board and Tract Society in the nation's giant crime have brought upon his head a storm of obloquy, the clergy and the representative men of his own denomination and of others in fellowship with it, have with almost no exception stood aloof or joined his enemies. When, a few weeks ago, he was invited, by a number of the most respectable citizens of New York and Brooklyn, to repeat, at the Cooper Institute, a series of masterly discourses which he had delivered in his own Church, showing that, in the words of his inviters, "Christianity is irreconcilably at war with such

Slavery as exists in our country, and any true and pure Church is necessarily its antagonist, and that it is the imperative duty of the organized Christianity of the land to war against it systematically and uncompromisingly, so long as it shall continue to exist," of the many "evangelical" clergymen of those cities, only three joined in the invitation. Of these, but one, HENRY WARD BEECHER, is at all conspicuous in his denomination, and he is deemed, by those who fill the chief seats in the synagogues, but little better than a heretic. The press, too, like the clergy of these sects, sides not with CHEEVER, but with his adversaries. The New York *Independent*, treacherous to the cause which it pretends to serve, is no exception to this statement. Yet Dr. CHEEVER's "Orthodoxy" is unquestionable; his deep sincerity and self-sacrificing devotion no man can deny; he belongs to no "infidel" Anti-Slavery Society, as ours has been, often, slanderously called; and his brethren in *theological* faith would seem to have no reason for refusing to assist him in his warfare against Slavery, except a want of real earnest sympathy with his *Anti-Slavery* faith and purpose.

Beside these facts we set another. The Boston *Courier* tells us that among the crowd assembled on the evening of the 28th of March, at Essex Street Church, in Boston, to congratulate the Rev. Dr. ADAMS, of "South-side" notoriety, on the completion of twenty-five years of service as the pastor of that Church, were nearly a hundred clergymen. Their presence was of course accepted, and no doubt intended, as attesting their respect for the reverend eulogist of Slavery, as a worthy brother in the Christian ministry. Not that they all agreed with him in his opinions of the patriarchal system; but only that his holding and expressing such opinions, whitening the loathsome sepulchre so full of all uncleanness, casting his influence on the side of those who turn God's children into working tools or worse, is no sufficient reason for refusing him that ministerial fellowship which, should he drop some doctrine from his creed, they would withdraw at once, however pure his life, and practically excellent his preaching. The bearing of the representatives of the popular religion toward Dr. CHEEVER and Dr. ADAMS respectively, tells a plain tale to those who have ears to hear.

"A Convention of Christian brethren" met in Worcester, Mass., on the 1st of March, and on the 2d, formed a "Church

Anti-Slavery Society," avowedly "to place the Church in its true position in relation to this great problem of our land and age." Its principles, as set forth in its Preamble and Declaration, are but in part those of our Society. Though six or seven States, and at least four denominations, were represented there, it enrolled but forty-four members, and eight or nine of these opposed affirming, in the Preamble, the "inherent sinfulness of Slaveholding." One minister declared that if those words should be inserted, but one of the seventeen members of the Association to which he belongs would come into the movement. They "would exclude him, and nineteen twentieths," he believed, "of the ministers of New England." Among the seven letters, received from persons who had been invited but could not be present, was one from a New Hampshire clergyman who "felt that here is the great difficulty—to bring the Church of Christ, in this country, to a right position in regard to the sin of Slavery. The Tract Society, at New York, and the New York *Observer*, represent in this respect, but too nearly, a large part of the Church." Yet he calls that "the Church of Christ," which is so reluctant to take right ground as to the *sin* of Slavery. One of the resolutions, unanimously adopted by the Society, appears to us open to question if not to censure, as liable at least to be understood as lowering the standard set up in the Declaration. It speaks of "honest differences of opinion among Anti-Slavery Christians in regard to the Bible view of Slavery." We are not willing to believe that this was meant to recognize the Anti-Slavery and Christian character of those who hold that the Bible contains a divine sanction of Slavery; but will not those who wish for countenance in such a belief be likely so to understand it? The resolution also seems to treat "the American Tract Society, at Boston," as an ally in the Anti-Slavery warfare; for it instructs the Executive Committee to confer with that Society, about the publishing of tracts to diffuse information touching the Bible view of Slavery and the duty of Christians in regard to it. It may be said, this does not necessarily imply allowance of the claims of that Society to public confidence in any other than a business character; treating it only as a publishing house with which an advantageous contract may be made for printing and distributing tracts. We think that it *does* mean more than this; this seems to us not the most obvious and natural construction of the act, and we have scarce a doubt it will be generally taken to mean more. But we have referred to this new Society, less for the purpose of criticising its position or its action, — in both of which some mixture of motive is perceptible, — than of presenting it as "a touchstone to the Churches," to prove how much, or little, vital Anti-Slavery is in them. From the small number of "evangelical" church members who have as yet participated in the movement, and from the difficulty which we are informed the worthy Secretary of the Society encounters in his efforts to enlist the churches and their pastors in its favor, we cannot help inferring that the event will warrant the erasure of "perhaps" from the following sentence which we quote from him: "Perhaps the fact will prove also to be, that the Church Anti-Slavery Society, with its acknowledged Christian basis in the Word of God, and with the acknowledged Christian character and standing of its founders and members so far, *is no more the representative or exponent of the visible American Church than the American Anti-Slavery Society is.*"

We add a testimony which may bear upon this point; premising that the Church Anti-Slavery Society is expressly pledged, by the Preamble to its Constitution, to "remember those that are in bonds as bound with them," and holds, in its Declaration of Principles, that "the Church and the Ministry are to form the conscience of the nation in respect to Slavery, and to make it loyal to the law of God." The Boston *Congregationalist*, a leading organ of the sect whose name it bears, claims, we believe, to be an Anti-Slavery paper of the right sort of Anti-Slavery; and claims, too, that "the great mass of the New England ministry and churches is Abolitionist, in the sense of being *principled* against Slavery, and desirous of its speediest possible abolition." But, in repelling the false charge of a New York paper, self-styled Christian, that "the three thousand New England clergymen have long been preaching almost nothing but Abolitionism," the *Congregationalist* says, "the entire 'three thousand' probably have never averaged more than one sermon a year upon that subject."

The separation of the Northern from the Southern Conferences of the Methodist Protestant Church, which in our last Report was mentioned as in prospect, has been accomplished.

In last November, a Convention of the Northern Conferences met at Cincinnati, and with only two dissenting votes, resolved, in the name of the Conferences represented, "that all official connection, coöperation, and official fellowship with and between said Conferences, and such Conferences and Churches, within the Methodist Protestant Association, as practice or tolerate Slaveholding and Slavetrading, be now and forever suspended." The seceding Conferences, it is said, are taking steps to form a union with the Wesleyans.

The Universalists, at their United States Convention, held in Providence, last fall, unanimously "resolved that we view with alarm the continued claims of the Slave Power to hold the children of Africa in bondage; that all such claims are contrary to the spirit of the Gospel; that we deplore the public demoral-ization which could originate such demands; reiterate our unqualified condemnation of Slavery, and reässert our determi-nation to labor for the maintenance of free institutions."

THE TRACT SOCIETIES.

The American Tract Society, at its last Annual Meeting, on the 12th of May last, by an overwhelming majority, approved the action of its Executive Committee in disregarding the remon-strances made to them, and refusing to publish anything relating to Slavery, — even to "discuss in a fraternal and Christian spirit," as recommended by the famous fourth resolution of 1857, "those moral duties which grow out of the existence of Slavery, and those moral evils and vices which it is known to promote, and which are condemned by Scripture and deplored by evangelical Christians." A resolution, moved by Dr. TYNG, to reäffirm the recommendation of the previous year, was laid on the table — virtually *under* it — by a vote of about three to one. A motion "that no tract bearing on the relation of Mas-ter and Slave be issued now, and that the circulation of the tract 'Sambo and Toney' [a Pro-Slavery tract,] be therefore stopped," was also voted down by a very large majority. A resolution offered by JOHN JAY, "that nothing published by this Society shall countenance the idea that the Scriptures sanc-tion the lawfulness of Slavery," was laid upon the table by an

16

equally decisive vote. Every living member of the old Board of Officers was reëlected, and in the place of two deceased Vice Presidents, Pro-Slavery men were chosen. Dr. ADAMS, of the South-side View, was put again on the Publishing Committee, by more than eight to one, and in direct contempt of a request from the "American Tract Society at Boston,"—the earlier Tract Society—that the New England member of that Committee might be chosen from its own Committee. On every contested point the victory of the Pro-Slavery party was complete; so signal that the sedate New York *Observer*, in the glow of exultation over it, grows hyperbolical, and pronounces it "the greatest moral victory of truth over error achieved since the Reformation under Martin Luther."

Not much would have been gained for right and freedom, if the other party had prevailed in everything on which they were agreed. At meetings which they held for consultation, on the 10th and 11th, the tone of sentiment was little higher than at the general meeting. They did not even propose to displace the officers who had "disappointed" them by failing to obey the fourth resolution of 1857, "the *honored brethren* who had committed an *error* in repressing truth." Dr. BACON thought "the Society might be put right without removing its officers." Dr. SMITH "entertained the *highest esteem* for the Executive Committee, personally, however much he might dissent from their views." Dr. HAWES "was behind no one in respect for the Secretaries and Committees." Dr. TYNG was "unalterably fixed" in favor of "a quiet and unopposed reëlection of the present officers, *in the confidence that they will decidedly and consistently carry out* the entire action of the Society at the meeting of 1857." He "considered the nine resolutions" of that meeting, [copied in our last Report] "appropriate, just, true, and likely to meet the views of Christians everywhere." Dr. THOMPSON, [of the Tabernacle Church, in New York, which, though professing some sort of Anti-Slavery, has still its negro pew] "was satisfied with both the negative and affirmative aspects of the fourth resolution, and would make no addition to it." A resolution, offered by LEWIS TAPPAN, requiring the Executive Committee to publish "a tract on the sinfulness of Slavery," was rejected; as was also an amendment which he proposed, to engraft a declaration of the sinfulness of Slavery on a resolution offered by Dr. Thompson, reäffirming the fourth resolution of 1857, and declaring that it ought to be carried into effect the present year. Dr. Bacon "had no doubt that this gigantic evil is sin, but it is a political question, and the less the Society meddles with political questions, the more good it will do." Dr. Smith "did not believe the mere legal relation of Slaveholder to Slave to be sin." Rev. Mr. Bishop, of Vermont, "wanted no Anti-Slavery discussion. The churches of Vermont wish simply to have the fourth resolution reäffirmed." Rev. Mr. Ide, of Massachusetts, "believed Slaveholding to be a sin, but is it necessary to say so on this occasion?" Rev. Mr. Moore agreed with Mr. Ide. S. B. Chittenden thought "a declaration that Slavery is sin, would only tear the Society to pieces." Dr. Hawes said "the Tract Society is not an Anti-Slavery Society." Rev. Mr. Smith thought that saying Slavery is sin "would defeat everything." Dr. Palmer feared defeat "if the outside question" should be "mingled with that of the duties of Slaveholders to their Slaves. He wished the Society to publish on the 'Duties of Masters.'" Dr. Proudfit "did not believe in interfering with the economics of the subject; the South would not bear that, *nor would we*. But a Christian presentation of the duties of masters should be made." Dr. Tyng thought "the word Slave might be dropped, and the duties of masters to servants might be taught; or, taking the extreme ground, that Slaves are chattels, we may still teach the duties of a man to his beast." [But suppose the "beast" is a stolen one; is not the "duty" to be preached in that case the very obvious duty of immediately restoring *it* to the rightful owner?] Rev. Mr. Bartlett thought "the reäffirmation of the fourth resolution of last year would accomplish the end desired, and to attempt more would defeat it." Rev. Mr. Patton, of Chicago, said "the feeling in the West is that Slavery is a sin. Whether anything need be added to the fourth resolution, of last year, to make it mean that, is a question." Dr. Cheever, Rev. H. T. Cheever, Lewis Tappan, and one or two others, were in favor of explicitly denouncing Slavery as sinful, but they were, proportionally, as much outnumbered in the conference of the minority, as that minority was in the meeting of the whole Society.

At the Annual Meeting of the Boston American Tract So-

ciety, on the 24th and 25th of May, the time was mostly given
to discussing and deciding what it ought to do in consequence
of the recent action of the other Tract Society. GARDNER G.
HUBBARD, Esq., presented a preamble and resolutions, setting
forth the views and purposes of those who disapproved that action.
The preamble stated that the course of the New York Society,
at its last meeting, had "impaired the union of feeling and
operation" for the sake of which the Societies became connected; that the wishes of the Boston Society in relation to the
choice of the Publishing Committee had been disregarded, contrary to the understanding upon which the union was effected;
and that "while we entertain great regard for the American
Tract Society of New York, and respect the wisdom and fore-
sight that have generally characterized its doings, yet we are
persuaded that greater efficiency can be imparted to the Tract
system by a return to the original status of the Society." The
first resolution was, "that we are no longer a branch of the
American Tract Society of New York, our union having been
virtually dissolved by its recent action." This was vigorously
opposed, and, after much debate, and at the earnest entreaty of
Dr. HUMPHREY, Dr. BACON, Dr. TYNG, WILLIAM ROPES, (officially the oldest member of the Board,) JOHN TAPPAN, the President, and other influential members, and the suggestion that,
perhaps, the New York Society would retract its error by another year, the friends of the resolution yielded, and in its place
was adopted one referring the expediency of dissolving the connection to the Executive Committee, to report next year. So
the partisans of the New York Society were permitted to pre-
vail on the most important point at issue. The other resolutions — adopted by a large majority — were, in substance, that
the Society would collect funds, and disburse them by its own
officers; that the Executive Committee procure "pious and useful books and tracts from such sources as may seem to them
expedient;" and that the resolutions of the New York Investi-
gating Committee of 1857 be heartily adopted and carried into
effect. A motion, that the Treasurer should pay no more money
to the New York Society, was modified with the mover's assent, so as to *except what should be paid for books and tracts;*
showing that one of the contemplated sources of supply was
the depository of that Society; and that the Boston was still

to be in fact, and not in name alone, a branch of the New York
Society. No wonder, therefore, that the sympathizers with the
latter claimed that, "in the main design of the Boston meeting,
the agitators were signally defeated." The choice of officers
came next. All the old officers were reëlected except SETH
BLISS, the Secretary, who had been active, unscrupulous, and
thorough-going in defence of the New York Society; and had,
besides, by some means, alienated a portion of his own party
from himself. But the Society took care to break the force of
any rebuke which this rejection might imply for his past course,
by a unanimous vote of thanks for his long and faithful services,
and a declaration of affection and respect for him. No one proposed that tracts be published against Slavery; and in assigning
reasons for a change of relation to the New York Society,
nothing, we see, is said of its infidelity to truth and righteousness in the matter of the nation's greatest sin; nothing of any
purpose or desire to deal with that sin more faithfully; not even
a hint or implication which goes further than proposing to
"*discuss* in a *fraternal* spirit" — fraternal, as is evidently meant,
toward those who turn their brothers into brutes — "the duties
growing out of the existence of Slavery, and the evils it is
known to promote;" leaving the *promoting* evil free from question, or questioned, at the most, by inference only. Such is
the action of the Boston Tract Society; and, of this, the editor
of the *Congregationalist,* himself one of the chief actors in it,
says, "The great body of the New England churches and ministry — *who do not desire to make the Tract Society a method
of Anti-Slavery attack,* on the one hand, but who cannot consent to have it compelled to silence with reference to the
sins inherent in, and growing out of Slavery, on the other
— we think will be, *and ought to be, satisfied* with this result."
We fear that the first half of this opinion is correct; — that
many "will be satisfied" because they wish to take no higher
ground than is here taken; and many others, perhaps, because
they honestly believe that some important advance has now
been made from the position of the New York Society. To the
latter class we would commend the Address put forth by the
Executive Committee of the Boston Society, in July last, which
testifies that "the organic relations of this Society to the New
York Society have not been materially changed;" that "we

invite no separation from that Society, but, under present circumstances, we believe the greatest amount of good will be done by each Society occupying the whole country as its field;" that "we are not an Anti-Slavery Society, but simply a Religious Tract Society;" [as if a true religion were not necessarily Anti-Slavery, and religious instruction for a people implicated in Slaveholding were not sadly incomplete with Anti-Slavery omitted or left to be inferred;] that "two Societies now offer their facilities for conveying the gospel of Christ in this form, to those who so much need" it; adding, "let each disciple of Christ choose his channel and employ it." So the New York Society is duly certified to the Christian public, as, equally with the Boston, a "channel" for conveying the gospel of Christ; and equally worthy to be employed by Christ's disciples. Of course the difference between the two touches no vital point of Christian duty. Let those who believe in a Christianity which is distinctly, actively, uncompromisingly Anti-Slavery, judge if they are not both unworthy of support and confidence. But we must not omit to mention that the Boston branch has lately published two tracts touching Slavery; one from a southern source, Pro-Slavery, on the "Scripture Duties of Masters," — with a prefatory disclaimer, by the Society, of responsibility for its doctrines; — the other, " Slavery and the Bible," representing the Bible, Christ, and the Apostles as in favor neither of perpetual Slavery nor immediate Abolition, but of some intermediate course, (unspecified,) whenever the lapse of time shall have rendered it "less likely to excite prejudice."

The American Board.

At the Annual Meeting of the American Board, held at Detroit on the 7th and next three days of September, the Slavery question, coming up with that of the Indian Missions, was speedily and quietly disposed of. The part of the Annual Report relating to the Indian Missions was referred to a Committee of which the Rev. Dr. BACON was Chairman; and his brief Report thereon was adopted unanimously, without debate. Its prominent points are these. The missionaries among the Choctaws are in a position " of much difficulty and peril." For "there has been, among the religious bodies" of the neighboring States, "a lamentable defection from some of the most elementary ideas of Christian morality, insomuch that Christianity has been represented as the warrant for oppression, and Christ as the minister of sin." [Finally adopted in a form more specific, but less forcible, thus:— "Insomuch that Christianity has been represented as the warrant for a system of Slavery which offends the moral sense of the Christian world, and thereby Christ has been represented as the minister of sin."] The missionaries "are in ecclesiastical relations" with these "religious bodies;" they "are watched by the upholders of Slavery," thereabouts, "ready to seize the first opportunity" to drive them from their field; they are charged by their enemies "with what are" there "called the dangerous doctrines of Abolitionism;" and in other quarters "with the guilt of silence in the presence of a hideous wickedness." It is "desirable that the Board should be relieved, as early as possible, from" these "unceasing embarrassments and perplexities." The time is not far distant when the Indians "will stand in the same relation to the missionary work as the white people in the adjacent States, and the Churches there will be the subject of home missionary, more properly than foreign missionary, patronage."

It will be seen that while the Report confesses that the missionaries are in ecclesiastical relations with religious bodies which "represent Christianity as a warrant for Slavery and Christ as the minister of sin," it has no word of censure for the missionaries, on that account; no hint of a disapproval of their holding such relations, or of a wish that they should cease to do so. The Board is exercised not about the wrongfulness of their position, as religious associates of those who have fallen away "from some of the first and most elementary ideas of Christian morality;" but about the difficulty and peril they encounter among such associates, with enemies in those regions seeking occasion against them as suspected Abolitionists, and charges coming from elsewhere that they do not speak out as they ought against "a hideous wickedness." It shows anxiety, not to have its missionaries bear a clear, decided testimony against "a system which offends the moral sense of the Christian world," nor to have its mission churches purified and kept pure from the pollution of such a system; but "to be relieved as early as possible from the embarrassments and perplexities connected with" its Indian Missions. And this relief it proposes to seek, not by insisting that its missionaries shall apply the gospel, in their preaching and the discipline of their churches, to the sin most easily besetting their hearers and professing converts; leaving the responsibility of refusal to do this upon the missionaries if they choose to take it, or of the consequences of their compliance upon those who, it is feared, will make that an occasion for expelling them; and trusting all results to Him whose bidding is, "Speak my words, whether they will hear or will forbear," speak, though it be to "a rebellious house," and fear not, "though thou dwellest among scorpions;" in short, not by fidelity to duty and firm faith in God; but, by deserting the post of "difficulty and peril," resigning all control and supervision of the missions in which, with its connivance, has grown up an evil it has not courage now to grapple with. For eleven years it has sustained its missionaries in that field, knowing from their own avowal that they would "not exclude a member from a mission church merely for being a Slaveholder;" nor "make it a condition of admission that a candidate should express a determination not to live and die a Slaveholder;" nor exercise discipline for the buying or selling of Slaves, except in *flagrant* cases of *manifest* disregard to the Slave's welfare; nor "make it a general rule to discipline for the separation of parents and children by sale or purchase." It knew, four years ago, that the Cherokee and Choctaw mission churches contained thirty-seven Slaveholders, and that if the missionaries themselves did not hold Slaves, they claimed the right to employ Slave labor at their own discretion, although admitting "the inexpediency of" their employing it except "in cases of manifest necessity;" and in this state of things it acquiesced. Thus has the Board connived at Slaveholding without limit of duration, and at Slavetrading without respect to the sanctity of domestic rights, in the very bosom of the churches it has called into being; and thus has it given countenance to that "defection" of the neighboring religious bodies, whereby "Christianity is represented as the warrant for oppression, and Christ as the minister of sin." And now that the growing Anti-Slavery sentiment of the North makes itself more distinctly felt, and "silence in the presence of the hideous wickedness" of Slavery is condemned, and "embarrassment and perplexity" can no longer be shunned by yielding to the *Southern* pressure, the Board thinks it is nearly time for "foreign" to give place to "home missionary patronage;"—in other words, is ready to resign its Indian missions to the watch and care of those "religious bodies" in the neighboring States, whose "lamentable defection from the elementary ideas of Christian morality" it attests. And *so* it is to be "relieved from its embarrassment!" When, after having helped to educate the Cherokees and Choctaws in a Pro-Slavery religion, it shall have passed them on to openly avowed Pro-Slavery spiritual guidance, the Board will lift its newly-washed hands and say, "I am clean from all complicity with Slaveholding. I have no mission churches open to the entrance of Slaveholders and Slave Traders; no missionaries who cite Jesus and the Apostles to sanction Slavery and the Slave Trade in the bosom of the Christian Church. Verily I have cleansed my heart, and washed my hands in innocency." And if some future POMROY, going on its errands into foreign lands, to spread its praises and increase its wealth, shall meet recorded proof of its connivance at the sin of Slavery, his answer will be ready,—"*that* belongs to the past and not the present history of the Board."

FOREIGN INTELLIGENCE.

Another national testimony has been borne, during the past year, against the Slave system. The little group of nations, claiming to be civilized, which still uphold within their borders or dependencies this concentration of essential barbarism, loses another member. Almost alone even now, the boastful North American Republic bids fair to be entirely so, ere long, as a Slaveholding and Slavery-upholding nation. The King of Portugal has sent out a proclamation, abolishing Slavery at Macao and Angola, and instituting a system of gradual emancipation in all the Portuguese Colonies — all children hereafter born in Slavery to become free on reaching the age of twenty.

From notices scattered through the newspapers of the past year, we perceive that the Russian Government is making steady progress in its measures for the emancipation of the serfs. Some

17

notion of the magnitude of this work is given by a table of
statistics, which appeared, last summer, in the New York *Herald*,
translated from a Belgian paper. According to this, which counts
the males alone, the serfs owned by private citizens are nearly
eleven millions; the Crown peasants, more than nine millions;
the peasants of the appanages, or lands of the Imperial family,
over seven hundred thousand, and some smaller classes, added
to these, make up a grand total of about twenty-four millions.
Reckoning the females at an equal number, the whole serf population counts not less than forty-eight millions. An estimate
made in 1836 gives nearly half a million more. A letter from
St. Petersburg, dated June 30, 1858, contains a list of thirty-
eight governments which had then commenced the formation
of Committees of emancipation, and in which more or less progress had been made in their deliberations. These governments
include within their bounds about ten million male serfs. About
the same time, a Vienna correspondent of the London *Times*
said "we learn from St. Petersburg, that the social reforms in
Russia are progressing surely, though slowly. Formerly the
Grand Duke Constantine was opposed to the plans of the Emperor, but his opinions have recently undergone a change."

On a journey which the Emperor made to Warsaw, last fall,
he addressed the nobles in the several governments through
which he passed, exhorting them to diligence in promoting the
great reform, and commending or reproving, as their zeal or slackness merited. To the nobles of the government of Tver, he said,
"I have confided to you a work, one of the most important to you
and to myself, the improvement of the condition of the peasants. I hope that you will justify my confidence. You know
how much I have your welfare at heart; but I hope, also, that
the interest of your peasants is dear to you. * * * * * It
is impossible for us not to proceed harmoniously in our acts,
since our sole desire is the general welfare of Russia." At Kos-
troma, he said, "I thank you for the zeal with which you have
anticipated my desire to improve the condition of the peasants.
This question, so seriously affecting Russia's future, moves me
to the heart. I hope you will justify my expectation in this,
which is in a manner a vital question, by adapting to the local
wants the fundamental principles enunciated in my rescripts,
and by terminating, with God's aid, this work, without detri-

ment to yourselves or to the peasants!" The nobility of Nijni Novgorod he thanked "for having been the first to respond" to his expectation, "in the grave question touching the improvement of the lot of the peasantry." Exhorting them to abandon selfish views, commending them for having "considerably advanced the work," he added, "if you prepare this great work conscientiously, and bring it to a happy issue, you will give me fresh proof of your attachment, and of your devotedness to the public weal." At Moscow, he had occasion to speak somewhat sharply. "To my great regret," he said, "I cannot thank you. Two years ago, I spoke to you of the necessity of proceeding, sooner or later, to the reform of those laws which regulate servitude — a reform *which must come from above, that it may not come from below.*" [A hint which the Slaveholding aristocracy of our own country would do well to heed.] "My words have been ill understood. Since then, this reform has been the object of my constant solicitude, and having invoked the Divine blessing on my undertaking, I have commenced the work. * * * * * I expected the nobility of Moscow would be the first to answer my appeal. But the nobles of Nijni Novgorod took the lead, and Moscow figures neither in the second nor third rank. I have felt great sorrow at this, because I love Moscow as my native city. I have fixed for you the bases of the reform, and I *shall never swerve from them.* * * * * You, yourselves, in your own interest, ought to endeavor to improve the condition of the peasants. * * * * * Do you understand me, gentlemen?" They understood him, if we may credit the statement of a letter from St. Petersburg, on the 22d of November, that "the speech of the Emperor, at Moscow, produced an excellent effect. The nobles learned from it that emancipation is irrevocably determined on." The same letter states that "while the great measure of liberation is going on, the Emperor has, in spite of all opposition, emancipated all the peasants on the appanages, or lands of the Imperial family, comprising several hundred thousand souls." The Director of the "Department of the Appanages," tried to dissuade the Emperor from so prompt an adoption of this measure, telling him "the lot of those peasants was so happy under his administration, that not one of them would take the liberty granted by the ukase." The Emperor's answer will suit quite as well another meridian, where it is fashionable to say "the Slaves are contented and happy, and wouldn't take freedom if it were offered." He said, "so much the better, if they remain in their villages, but *we shall nevertheless have done our duty* if we treat them with humanity." The event, however, proved that even well-treated bondmen love liberty too well to accept Slavery, even with kind usage, when they can be free. The ukase had scarcely appeared, when the peasants, by a general movement, hastened "to inscribe themselves as willing to change their condition." Another letter of the same date, from St. Petersburg, says, "the question of emancipation, so far as it depends upon the Emperor, is getting on rapidly. He has just ordered that the serfs belonging to the mines, under the direction of the Minister of Finance, be freed in six months, and three Committees have been organized to carry this order into effect." A letter from the same place, on the 27th of November, mentions that the Committee of St. Petersburg had finished its deliberations, and presented their results to the Emperor. We gather from his speeches to the nobles, that when the reports of all the governments shall have come in, two delegates from each Committee are to meet at St. Petersburg, and, as a general Committee, revise all the various propositions, and complete a definite plan. It is said that all the plans discussed may be included in two classes; the one conforming to the Imperial rescript, which, as we stated in our last report, proposes a "transition state," to continue not longer than twelve years; the other calling for "complete, immediate emancipation," as attended with less danger than "transitory situations." We need not say which seems to us the wiser proposition.

A recent number of the London *Anti-Slavery Advocate* brings us intelligence of a movement, just beginning in Great Britain, for the formation of a National Anti-Slavery League. The Edinburg Young Men's Anti-Slavery Society, at its last meeting, in March last, resolved to give its "strenuous support to the organization of a National Anti-Slavery League, with an annual conference, based upon the same principles as the American Anti-Slavery Society; the object of which League shall be to diffuse, organize, and direct the Anti-Slavery spirit of this country, and work out Great Britain's special province in the struggle; endeavoring, at the same time, to redouble the aid already given to our fellow-workers in America; and that the various Societies be addressed, and urged to take immediate steps in the matter."

Our cause has had a faithful and efficient representative in Great Britain, for the last few months, in the person of Miss SARAH P. REMOND. In public lectures and in private conferences, she has labored diligently and done good service; and while commending Anti-Slavery truth to the favorable regard of listening multitudes, or circles more select, has won for herself applause, and personal esteem and friendship wherever she has gone. Among the fruits of her successful efforts, we may reckon a donation of $100 from the Warrington Anti-Slavery Society to our Society; and the excellent Address of the inhabitants of Warrington and its neighborhood to the citizens of the United States, "agreed to at a crowded meeting held in the largest public room in the town," and signed by the Mayor, the Rector, the Member of Parliament for the borough, and more than thirty-five hundred of the inhabitants; more, by twelve hundred, it is stated, than ever, in that place, signed any previous address or petition. As the Address is brief we copy it entire.

"The principle that man cannot hold property in man appears to us so reasonable, and of such universal application, that we are ready, at first, to believe it must also be of universal practice. But when we are painfully reminded that in America, men and women, of like passions with ourselves, are bought and sold, and treated as chattels, it is difficult to reduce our remonstrances to a set form. We think nature herself should resent the outrage. It is hard to coin our hearts into arguments, to twist our feelings into logic, and with words to vindicate the stamp of God.

Inasmuch, however, as Slavery has grown up through generation after generation, as an Institution of America, and as thus what is an outrage may be looked upon as a product of nature, we will attempt to frame an appeal.

By our common humanity, which Slavery insults — by the one origin, one probation, and one end of all men, be they black or white — by that one God who sits above the consciences of all as universal Lord — and by that final account which, without distinction of Master or Slave, we must all render up at the great day — by these considerations we appeal to you — to you who now ply this unlawful traffic, that you relinquish it forever; — and to you who are engaged in the noble work of Abolition, that you go forward, conscious that you have with you the great heart of England, that, in your highest enthusiasm, keeps equal pulse with yours — and, if it were allowed to speak out, the great heart of man.

We make this appeal, not in the spirit of dictation, but of friendship. We recognize the common brotherhood of all men; and this appeal is lodged with our white brother on behalf of him who is no less our brother, and whose equality, as it is established in nature, we would desire to see established in universal recognition."

A letter from the Secretary of the Warrington Anti-Slavery Society, accompanying the Address, says, "Miss REMOND's exertions have been eminently serviceable by stimulating into more active life the existing sentiment of our town. * * * * * The strong conviction of injustice attendant upon the system of Slaveholding is too indelibly stamped upon the national mind ever to be effaced, and there only needs some exciting cause to evidence its vitality."

The Protestants of Belgium have also sent their word of gentle, earnest, eloquent admonition to those in this land, who, while calling themselves Christians, hold, or help to hold Christ in Slavery, in the persons of his dark-hued brethren. It is addressed in terms "TO THE CHRISTIANS OF THE UNITED STATES WHO SUPPORT SLAVERY;" and uses such a force of argument, persuasion, warning, and entreaty, as we see not how any who deserve the name of Christian, can gainsay or resist.

OBITUARY.

Again we have to mourn the loss of faithful and beloved co-workers, taken from among us since our last yearly gathering. In the death of ELLIS GRAY LORING, Esq., of Boston, on the 24th of May last, at the age of fifty-five years, the Anti-Slavery cause was — to human apprehension many years too soon — bereft of one of its earliest, worthiest, and most honored friends. We cannot, in the space at our command, if it were possible, indeed, in any space, render in words a fitting tribute to his worth, or do full justice to the high esteem, the warmth of personal regard, and strength of friendly attachment, which his rare blending of amiable and noble qualities elicited from us and all who knew him well; nor tell his gentleness, his truth in every

trial, his sound integrity, quiet firmness, courteous speech and
bearing, his moral courage and almost excessive modesty, his
warm affection, sterling sense, and calm, deliberate wisdom, his
delicacy, refinement, tenderness of soul, averse to controversy
and shrinking from public notice, yet coupled with a conscien-
tiousness and strong humanity which made him sacrifice his
tastes and feelings, the instincts of his sensitive, retiring nature,
to brave conspicuity, reproach, and strife, and risk social position
and professional success, in serving the imperilled right, and
testifying for unpopular and persecuted truth, and helping the
outcast and despised.   When Mr. GARRISON began this movement for the Slaves' deliverance, and few were at once enlightened, honest, and bold enough to show themselves upon his
side, he was among those few.   He was found in the little company which met in the vestry of the colored people's church in
Belknap street, Boston, to deliberate on the formation of a New
England Anti-Slavery Society; and though at first he hesitated
as to the expediency of taking ground expressly for "*immediate
emancipation*," his clear discernment and fidelity to right would
not permit him long to hesitate; and having once subscribed
that vital article of our Anti-Slavery faith, he was true to it till
death; and was among the most efficient members of the
organization formed to uphold it.   For many years he was a
Manager of that Society, and to him his associates could ever
look with confidence for the soundest judgment and most trust-
worthy counsel.   In his profession as a lawyer, too, he found
and used occasions to serve the cause of freedom.   His name is
honorably associated with the case which gave the Supreme
Court of Massachusetts an opportunity to affirm the right of a
Slave to freedom, when brought by his pretended owner into
Massachusetts; — one step toward that position which that and
every other so-called Free State must yet take in order to be
truly free,— that, brought or coming of his own accord, no human being shall continue a Slave a moment after he has touched
its soil and breathed its air.   To Mr. LORING's zeal and earnest
devotion and legal skill and ability is due, in no small degree,
the right decision of that case, which not only secured to little
Med her freedom, but established an important legal principle,
as a breakwater against the rising tide of Slaveholding aggression.   He bore his testimony, too, against the prejudice which

proscribes the colored man from all but menial employments, by
setting the first example of educating for his own profession one
of that proscribed class.   When free speech and the right of
peaceably assembling to promote the cause of freedom were
menaced with prohibitory legislation at the hint of a time-serv-
ing Governor, Mr. LORING was prompt to "stand in the gap,"
and as one of those who went before the Legislative Committee
to protest against the meditated outrage, helped to prevent its
perpetration.   The infamous enactment of a Pro-Slavery Congress, which would have turned the whole North into a hunting-
ground for Slavecatchers, inspired in him neither respect nor
fear.   His roof gave shelter to Ellen Craft, when the base ministers of the lower law were seeking her to drag her back to Slavery.
Not least among the proofs he gave of self-forgetting faithful-
ness to the cause, was his continuing to act as one of the Finan-
cial Committee of the hated, dreaded, vilified *Liberator*, letting
his name appear in it in testimony thereof, from week to week,
up to the very last before the number which announced his
death.   Though for a few years past he was but seldom seen in
public Anti-Slavery gatherings, feeling that now his presence
was less needed there, yet he never lost his interest in the
cause, nor ceased in unconspicuous ways to serve it.   Nor has
he ceased to serve it yet.   The influence of his bright example
lives; the memory of his beautiful life, — of his words of truth
and deeds of goodness — is with us still to guide, inspire, and
strengthen, as we toil on a little longer, urging the cause he
loved each day still nearer to its certain final triumph.

On the 14th of last October, the Hon. WILLIAM JAY, long
and well known as among the most determined enemies of
Slavery, died at his residence, near Bedford, in Westchester
county, N. Y., at the age of sixty-nine years. As early as 1835,
when the violence of the Pro-Slavery mob in all parts of the
North was furiously striving to crush the Anti-Slavery movement in its infancy, he openly identified himself with it, publishing an able work in its behalf, and has ever since held fast
the faith he then avowed. He has, from time to time, made
valuable contributions to its literature, and in other ways has
aided to promote it. Though, from a difference on some points
as to measures, he ceased, some years ago, to be a member of
our Society, yet he was always one with it in principle, and felt

a deep interest in its doings, was a subscriber to its official organ, and a frequent welcome visitor at its office, to speak words of counsel and encouragement, which will not be soon forgotten, to those who labor in its service there. Inheriting a venerated name, and worthily upholding the honor it conferred, respected as a man and as a magistrate, giving the forces of a cultivated mind and a benevolent heart to various enterprises which aim at bettering the condition of mankind, as well as to the duties of his private and official stations, and thus achieving — what he well deserved — beside his other dignities, the reputation of a Christian philanthropist, he had a weight of influence to employ in favor of this cause, which few among its advocates can claim; and it is still more to his credit to have used it well than to have had it in so large amount. His faithful dealing with the Tract Society and kindred organizations, for their delinquency and treason to the right, is known to all who are familiar with the history of reform among us. But a few months before his death, he took occasion — from a request for pecuniary aid to an auxiliary of the American Tract Society — to bear anew his testimony against that body, in such terms as these: — "Belial may well be content that the Society shall, in the name of Christ, do battle against dancing, novel-reading, tobacco-chewing, &c., and even promulgate gospel doctrines, while it abstains from all assaults on his own favorite institution, comprising, as it does, the sum of all villanies. * * * * * The man who, by affirming the rightfulness of Slavery, confounds the moral sense, and subverts all moral distinctions, I denounce as a criminal against our common humanity, and wittingly or unwittingly, an enemy of Christ. Yet such a man the Tract Society delights to honor, and commits to him absolute censorship of the press." Judge JAY, moreover — judge as he was — knew well enough the relative authority of the higher and the lower law, to have no reverence for the statute which hounds on the kidnapper after his "legal" prey. His will contains a bequest to his son, JOHN JAY — the worthy almoner of such a bounty — of "$1000 in trust, to be applied, at his discretion, in promoting the safety and comfort of Fugitive Slaves." The blessing of them that were ready to perish shall come upon him, and the delivered bondman shall be the witness

18

for him when the judgment goes forth, "inasmuch as ye did it
to one of the least of these, ye did it unto me."

On the 13th of March, at Eagleswood, near Perth Amboy,
N. J., died ARNOLD BUFFUM, one of the veteran soldiers of the
Anti-Slavery warfare, in his seventy-eighth year. He was one
of the twelve who, in January, 1832, formed the New England
Anti-Slavery Society, of which he was the first President, and
the first lecturing agent. In the latter capacity he labored with
much zeal, and industry, and efficiency. He was a member, also,
of the Convention which, in December, 1833, formed the American Anti-Slavery Society, and affixed his name to its Declaration of Sentiments. After the secession of 1840, he ceased, for
a time, to act with our Society; not, as he often said, from want
of confidence in his old associates, but because he thought, in
his circumstances then, he could better serve the cause in connection with the new Society. However we may regret this
as an error of judgment, we doubt not that he acted conscientiously, and he certainly has not faltered in his testimony against
Slavery. The following extract from a letter, written to Mr.
GARRISON, on the 18th of last January, shows how he felt toward the organization he had helped to form twenty-five years
before. "Should an opportunity be permitted me, at the next
Annual Meeting of the American Anti-Slavery Society, I should
be happy to declare my unbroken unity with those who took the
lead in that modern revival of that work and labor of love, which
is now spreading a most hopeful and encouraging influence
throughout the civilized world; and which will certainly bring
the day when every yoke of bondage will be broken, and the
oppressed go free; when the whole world shall unite in the
observance of such a fast as God has chosen; and when we
all shall rejoice in the coming of 'an acceptable day to the
Lord.'"

He was a man of serene and cheerful temper, and his naturally buoyant spirit was sustained by a firm, religious faith. He
had a full belief in the brotherhood of man, and in the Father-
hood of God. He believed that the Almighty, as he had promised, would break the rod of the oppressor, and let the oppressed
go free. This belief animated him in his long-continued labors
in behalf of his fellow-men, and inspired him with unabated confidence in God. His last few years were spent with his chil-

dren and grand-children, at Eagleswood, where his life ebbed peacefully and happily away, and when the appointed hour had come, he gently yielded his breath, with the assurance that he was falling into his Heavenly Father's arms, and that a glorious future was before him. His surviving coadjutors in the cause of oppressed humanity will remember his untiring zeal, his indomitable courage, his unwearied diligence. The people of color will ever bear in mind his manly and unflinching advocacy of their rights. And none who knew him will ever lose the impression of his straightforwardness in every good work to which he was called.

And now, just as we are turning from the closing to the opening year, and girding up our strength for the toils and trials of a new campaign, Death makes another gap in our advancing column. No truer heart has ever beat in all its serried ranks, no braver spirit ever answered to the battle call of Freedom by leaping to her van, and meeting whatsoever fate awaits it there, than that true heart which has just ceased its beating; than that brave spirit which has just gone up from the forefront of our array. On the 28th of April, at the age of fifty-two, CHARLES F. HOVEY died in Boston. He had not been, like those of whom we have already spoken, among the first to enlist in the Anti-Slavery cause; but from the moment when its claims came clearly and distinctly to his moral vision, and constrained the assent of his whole spiritual nature, he has been found among its firmest friends, its boldest advocates, its most diligent promoters. A successful merchant, he held the wealth his industry and business talents had accumulated, as a sacred trust for universal humanity, and of course has made it tributary, in large measure, to this cause, which reaches down to humanity's lowest level to lift it up from uttermost debasement. A man of clear intellect, and honest heart, he saw the magnitude and bearing of the principles our work involves, and grasped them with a corresponding earnestness. Unfettered by forms, regardless of the *husks* of faith, he sought the living kernel, and made it fructify in practical beneficence. In the words of a just eulogy, pronounced at his funeral, "His integrity stood like the Alps; his benevolence was extended, diffusive, overflowing like the Nile; his philanthropy broad as the whole earth. His personal independence and moral courage were equal to any emergency;

he asked not what was popular, but only what was *right*. Simple and unpretending in his manners, unselfish in his aims, and transparent as a perfect mirror, he sought no distinction, and desired no conspicuity. In his feelings, principles, and conduct, he was thoroughly democratic, in the highest and noblest sense of that term. He was a hearty despiser of all shams; he abhorred the proscriptive spirit of caste, in every form; he saw through the frivolous distinctions and hollow conventionalities of society,—was of the people, with the people, and for the people, as against usurpation, oppression, and monopoly,—and with the poet Burns saw and affirmed —

> ' The rank is but the guinea's stamp,
> The man 's the gold, for a' that.'

Freedom was the element in which his spirit delighted to dwell, —that freedom which saves, elevates, and blesses all its recipients. With him, free inquiry, free speech, a free platform, free trade, were no rhetorical flourishes, no party catch-words, but vital principles, to be cherished, asserted, propagated, at all times, at whatever cost; and for their diffusion and vindication he was ever ready to take any risk, and to make any sacrifice.

"In all the relations of life, he was most exemplary—a model merchant, a devoted husband, a most affectionate father, a sterling friend. His religion was that of the Good Samaritan, and therefore unrecognized as religion by Priest and Levite. All forms of misery, destitution, and helplessness appealed to him for aid, and readily obtained it; for his benevolence was inexhaustible. If all who have been helped by his counsel, and blessed by his charity, were present on this occasion, the throng would be multitudinous. His removal will be felt as a general bereavement, and the tears of thousands in other parts of the country, who knew his worth by report, but were not personally acquainted with him, will freely mingle with the tears of his household and bosom friends. More even than this — the generous, intrepid, uncompromising friend and defender of the millions of manacled and dehumanized Slaves in our guilty land, as he was, they will constitute a vast procession to follow his remains to the grave, bewailing their loss."

That Mr. HOVEY was a most sincere and devoted, as well as generous friend of the Anti-Slavery cause, the following clause from his will, which we publish here in justice to his memory and character, abundantly shows:

ARTICLE 16. After setting aside sufficient funds to pay all legacies and bequests herein made, I direct my said Trustees to hold all the rest and residue of my estate, real, personal and mixed, in special trust for the following purposes, namely; to pay over, out of the interest and principal of said special trust, a sum of not less than eight thousand dollars annually, until the same be all exhausted, to said Wendell Phillips, William Lloyd Garrison, Stephen S. Foster, Abby K. Foster, Parker Pillsbury, Henry C. Wright, Francis Jackson and Charles K. Whipple, and their survivors and survivor, for them to use and expend, at their discretion, without any responsibility to any one, for promotion of the Anti-Slavery cause and other reforms, such as Woman's Rights, Non-Resistance, Free Trade and Temperance, at their discretion; and I request said Wendell Phillips and his said associates to expend not less than eight thousand dollars annually, by the preparation and circulation of books, newspapers, employing agents, and the delivery of lectures that will, in their judgment, change public opinion, and secure the abolition of Slavery in the United States, and promote said other reforms. Believing that the chain upon four millions of slaves, with tyrants at one end and hypocrites at the other, has become the strongest bond of the Union of the States, I desire said Phillips and his associates to expend said bequest by employing such agents as believe and practice the doctrine of "No union with slaveholders, religiously or politically"; and by circulating such publications as tend to destroy every pro-slavery institution.

AGENTS, PUBLICATIONS, &c.

We have but little space left in which to make a bare mention of the Society's operations during the year. In pursuance of its great object, the renewing of the national heart and conscience, so that the great wickedness of human Slavery may be repented of and put away, it has been instant, in season and out of season, in proclaiming those truths, principles, ideas, and facts, all which point directly to the Duty, the Policy, the Safety, and the Necessity of the entire abolition of Slavery in the country. In promulgating these truths, it has had as its agents, directly or indirectly, the following persons: PARKER PILLSBURY, and ANDREW T. FOSS, of New Hampshire; Rev.

N. R. Johnston, of the Reformed Presbyterian Church in Vermont; Charles C. Burleigh, of Connecticut; Charles K. Whipple, Charles L. Remond, Sarah P. Remond, Joseph A. Howland, and Frances H. Drake, of Massachusetts; Aaron M. Powell, Sallie Holley, Caroline F. Putnam, Susan B. Anthony, and Rev. William H. Fish, of New York; and Daniel S. Whitney, in Iowa, &c. The Society also had the frequent and invaluable aid, in public advocacy of its objects, of William Lloyd Garrison, Wendell Phillips, Esq., Rev. Theodore Parker, Rev. William H. Furness, Rev. T. W. Higginson, Rev. Adin Ballou, Rev. Samuel J. May, Edmund Quincy, Esq., Mrs. Lucretia Mott, J. Miller McKim, Stephen S. Foster, Ezra H. Heywood, William Wells Brown, Henry C. Wright, J. Symington Brown, G. B. Stebbins, Rev. C. B. Campbell, of Iowa, Marius R. Robinson, of Ohio, Rev. M. D. Conway, Rev. Frederick Frothingham, of Maine, and many others.

Numerous Meetings, and Conventions have been held in all parts of the Eastern, Northern, and Western States; the general arrangement and superintendence of which, as well as of the Society's publications, and of the distribution of the same, has been with the Acting General Agent, Samuel May, Jr.

Besides its Annual Reports for 1856, '57, '58, two reports in one pamphlet of 208 pages, — a document of great ability and value as a history of the cause during the two years from May, 1856 to May, 1858,— the Society has issued several small Tracts, large numbers of which were sold at cost, or gratuitously distributed. The principal of these are the following:

Great Auction Sale of Slaves (belonging to the Butler estate) at Savannah, Georgia. Reported for the *Tribune.*

Present Condition of the Free Colored People of the United States. By Rev. James Freeman Clarke.

Speech of Wendell Phillips, before the Committee on Federal Relations of the Massachusetts Legislature, in behalf of the Petition for a law against Slave-hunting.

No Fetters in the Bay State. Speech of William Lloyd Garrison, on the same occasion.

Speech of Charles C. Burleigh at the Annual Meeting of the Massachusetts Anti-Slavery Society. "No Slave-hunting in the Old Bay State."

SPEECH OF REV. HENRY BLEBY, Missionary to Barbadoes, on the Results of Emancipation in the British West India Colonies.·

SLAVERY AND THE AMERICAN BOARD OF COMMISSIONERS FOR FOREIGN MISSIONS. By Charles K. Whipple.

THE AMERICAN TRACT SOCIETY. By Charles K. Whipple.

PROCEEDINGS OF THE ANTI-SLAVERY CONVENTION IN WEST RANDOLPH, VERMONT, August, 1858.

In addition to the above, the Society has gratuitously distributed about 15,000 tracts and pamphlets, which, averaging ten pages each, amount to *one hundred and fifty thousand pages*.

The NATIONAL ANTI-SLAVERY STANDARD is the Society's organ. It is published weekly, in the city of New York, at No. 5 Beekman street. Subscription price, $2 per annum. OLIVER JOHNSON, Esq. Editor; assisted by a large corps of Associate Editors, and of Correspondents at home and abroad. Subscriptions, in Great Britain and Ireland, may be sent to RICHARD D. WEBB, 176 Great Brunswick street, Dublin.

The ANTI-SLAVERY BUGLE, the organ of the Western Anti-Slavery Society, is published at Salem, Columbiana Co., Ohio, at $1.50 per annum. B. S. JONES, Esq. Editor.

The LIBERATOR is published and edited by WM. LLOYD GARRISON, at No. 221 Washington street, Boston. Subscription, $2.50 per annum.

www.ingramcontent.com/pod-product-compliance
Lightning Source LLC
Chambersburg PA
CBHW030604270326
41927CB00007B/1035